NOT REALLY A
Princess

NICKI CORINNE WHITE
Put on a Heart of Compassion -- Colossians 3:12

Published by Carpenter's Son Publishing, Franklin, Tennessee
Published in association with
Larry Carpenter of Christian Book Services, LLC
of Franklin, Tennessee
Edited by Christi Callahan
Cover photo by Jamie Hudson Photography
Cover and Interior Design by
Debbie Manning Sheppard
ISBN:978-1-946889-24-9
Printed in the United States of America

NOT REALLY A

Princess

new

NICKI CORINNE WHITE

Put on a Heart of Compassion -- Colossians 3:12

ENDORSEMENTS

"Surviving rejection, neglect, and parental mental illness: Nicki Corinne White demonstrates God's faithful, healing hand of protection amid enduring personal hardship."

PATRICIA T. BOLIOU, M.A.,
LICENSED PROFESSIONAL COUNSELOR

"I was drawn in to Nicki's openness and raw authenticity in the telling of her story. She has a rough go of it... enduring things no little girl should have to endure. I did not detect bitterness or negativity in the relaying of her journey. In fact, just the opposite,; I was especially touched to hear her tell about the power of hope and the healing that comes from forgiveness and grace."

PAM STRAIN CO-AUTHOR,
SPIRITUAL SEEDS: How To Cultivate Spiritual Wealth Within Your Future Children
MENTOR, SPEAKER AND CO-FOUNDER OF LIFT

"I loved the book. It is written in such a soulful manner. It reminded me to be kind, notice the needs of those around me, and not forget to smile!"

RUTH MAYER
AMERICAN MASTER ARTIST

ENDORSEMENTS

"Nicki shares her story from the heart and with candid honesty. The story's not perfect, life's not perfect, but Jesus is. Read along and rejoice with Nicki in the hope and healing Christ brings."

KATHLEEN THOMSON
THE MASTER'S UNIVERSITY

*In **Not Really a Princess** Nicki White weaves her engaging personal story from painful struggles to hope. Orphaned, adopted, grieving, rejected, disappointed... all this is the background to a slow but sure path to faith and compassion for others. The God of grace is the hero of this story and with Nicki we learn many lessons about His purpose, care, forgiveness and restoration.*

PASTOR DONN MOGFORD
MINISTRIES REPRESENTATIVE
WEST, SHEPHERD'S MINISTRIES

DEDICATED TO

MOMA,

FRANCES DOYLE MAYNARD ~

God had a master plan for your life to be an example for others to see that there is a way through adversity—one of hardship, trials, and grief turned to love, joy, and encouragement.

TO LISA SHUMAKER ~

Never has there been a dearer sister. You have been there my entire life, watching out for both of us through death, poverty, and many trials. I can never thank you enough. God greatly blessed me with giving us each other.

TO MY HEAVENLY FATHER ~

Powerful, sovereign, merciful God, I am only a humble servant with a great desire for others to see the hope you give to us in difficult times. I am so thankful you chose me to share your message. I could not have finished this book without all factors coming together so beautifully. I have prayed for the past several years for the ability to share your words, not mine. Thank you for granting me this dream.

CONTENTS

ACKNOWLEDGMENTS

JESSICA EVERETT ~

I thank you so very much for helping week after week with this project, the blog, and the tech questions. I could not have done this without a helper.

NATHAN WHITE ~

Thank you for my website and all the wonderful insight into those techy things I am not prolific at. You are truly gifted.

RUTHANNE BEDDOE ~

You have always been an inspiration to me. Thank you for your editing and encouragement to get this project started and through to completion.

JAMIE HUDSON ~

Thank you for your beautiful photography and for patiently waiting, letting this long process work. I look forward to future projects.

ACKNOWLEDGMENTS

JESSICA OWINYO ~

Thank you for your brilliance in social media and being patient with me and all my tech questions.

AMY CRIST, JENISE SHUPE, SUSAN GREENE, CINDY FRENDT, CHRYSTAL KING ~

Thank you ladies for being on my jury team to let me know what needed work. It was an encouragement to me and spurred me on.

SAM SHUMAKER ~

Thank you for all your insights into this book and loving on Moma for so many years.

CRAIG WHITE ~

And I never could have done any of this without you allowing me to take my time with this. Thank you for your encouragements over the years and your patience with my tech questions. I love you, sweetheart.

LIST OF KEY CHARACTERS

FRANCES/MOMA ~
My adoptive mother whom I consider my true mom.

LISA ~
My sister that I grew up with. She is my half sister. We have the same mom and different dads. She has a husband, Sam, and three sons: Daniel, Jacob, and Scott.

SAMUEL/DAD ~
My adoptive dad.

GRANDMA ANNA MAE
AND GRANDPA ARCHIE ~
My grandparents who lived in a different house on our same farm.

PASTOR DARRELL ~
The pastor who officiated my dad's funeral. He moved to Boise, Idaho, several years later, and our family attended that church when we moved there.

LIST OF KEY CHARACTERS

WINNIE ~
My birth mother. I never met her,
but Lisa did on several occasions.

FRANK ~
My birth dad, whom I met in my thirties.

DON ~
My eldest brother that I met in my late twenties. He has a wife,
Moe, and two daughters: Melissa and Megan.

LARRY ~
My next eldest brother, whom I met when I met Don. He has a
wife, Diana, a daughter, Laura, and a son, Tavis.

SHANNON ~
My cousin adopted by my birth mom who became my sister.

MELINDA (KNOWN AS MEL) ~
My sister discovered after our birth mom died.
We are full sisters.

Cowgirls Lisa and Nicki

Brothers Don and Larry
with sister Mel

Lisa and Nicki
in Mukilteo, WA

Nicki and Lisa circa 1961 in Woodenville

*Pilchuck River
at the
Snohomish
Farm*

Lisa and Moma looking towards the lower field at the Snohomish Farm

Moma reading her Bible.

Moma praying just weeks before her death.

INTRODUCTION

Therefore, as God's chosen people,
holy and dearly loved, clothe
yourselves with compassion, kindness,
humility, gentleness and patience.

COLOSSIANS 3:12 NIV

Often, I don't even look at the introduction when I read a book. I dive right in without a thought. However, I have learned that it can be extremely helpful, and I hope this one gives you some insight into the journey ahead. I want this book to show you how three lives were thoroughly changed by God.

Every adopted woman feels as though she is a princess, or at least I did. Perhaps it was due to the hope that I held onto for so long—that the ideal parents were out there somewhere. Or maybe it was just the dream of a child.

For years, as my life unfolded, I had numerous friends who prodded me to write a book about my life. They believed my story was one that should be told. I agreed, and not only that; it is a story I *needed* to tell.

I began to consider it in my twenties. By the time I hit fortysomething, I knew in my heart it was time to tell my story. Yet I struggled with the fact that I did not have all the facts. Much of my life is a mystery that I was fearful of uncovering. I did not want to hurt my adoptive parents by searching out the unknown. When you are adopted, the family you are adopted into becomes your real family. You share their pain, joy, struggles, and failures.

Initially, I had no desire to find out anything about my heritage. And I was concerned because my story was not yet finished. There are so many missing pieces, and I have worried that I may remember something different than someone else. But after much contemplation, I decided I could not worry about that. This is *my* story, as I remember it. There have been twists and turns, and a bit of mystery about things not yet resolved. It is a puzzle without all the pieces, orchestrated by God and carefully crafted from hard times and unusual circumstances.

It is my hope that by reading about some of my pain and suffering, God can use my testimony to help you see His plan for your life. We all have things we can share, and we all have skeletons in our closet. We all experience the joy and pain of life which molds us into who we become. All of these things can bring about growth, though the process is sometimes hard. Thus far, my journey through life has involved adoption, grief, hurt, rejection, poverty, widowhood,

and discovery. I hope that, by sharing my experiences, you will be inspired to grow and change.

The lessons life taught me finally made me realize that I was not a princess from a faraway land. As a matter fact, I am far from it. There is no fabulous castle in my past, nor a home where everything was perfect. Oftentimes, we can thwart our joy by desiring a life different from the one we have. The struggles you encounter in life can be utilized to help form you into all that you can be, if you will choose joy over pain.

Life is a gift

*The two most important
days in your life are the day
you were born and the day
you find out why.*

MARK TWAIN

THE EARLY YEARS

*For he chose us in him before the
creation of the world to be holy and
blameless in his sight.*

EPHESIANS 1:4 NIV

*H*ave you ever thought about how your childhood laid the foundation for who you are? Have you considered how many aspects of your personality, including insecurities, passions, and dreams, were shaped by your childhood experiences?

For years I ignored the idea that any of my background affected me in any way. I have never wanted to make excuses for bad behavior. Only in the past ten years or so have I realized that my past *did*, in fact, mold me. That is not a bad thing. I just need to accept it.

There are things in life that hit us in the face, things that make us who we are. Sometimes they are twisted like a bad dream, and other times they go on and on, continuing our journey, growing us to become all we are to become.

My story begins in Woodinville, Washington, in the early 1960s. A small rural town in Western Washington, Woodinville is about twenty miles northeast of Seattle. I lived there on a small farm, along with my sister Lisa (pronounced "Lyssa"). I was just eighteen months old when we were adopted, and Lisa was close to three years old.

My dad, Samuel, stood six feet two with green eyes and almost-black hair the color of forged iron. Growing up, I heard many say he looked a lot like Chuck Conner with dark hair or perhaps Kirk Douglas. As I grew up, I could totally see those comparisons. He was a jack-of-all-trades, a gifted individual who was an entrepreneur before it was the trendy thing to be. My dad's hobby was horses. Although I was very young, I remember that Moma and Dad would take the horses on long trail rides or to horse shows on the weekends. My sister and I would usually stay with our grandparents. We would be all decked out in our boots, tassels, and cowboy hats. We also had wooden stick horses like all good cowgirls.

My moma, Frances, lived a difficult life and suffered much loss at an early age. She was five feet two with mink-colored hair and a fair complexion. Moma's dad died when she was only five years old. Her mom had to work to support them, so there was no time for Moma to be a little girl. Her mom had to work to support them, so there was no time for Moma to be a little girl. Grandma Anna Mae, my mom's mother, was a city official and worked many long hours. Because Grandma was away from home so much, my moma had to take care of her younger brother.

Years later, on November 23, 1939, Moma married Samuel. They met in Southwest Washington State and were married three months later. They wanted to have a family of their own, but after ten miscarriages, Moma and Dad decided to foster kids. I can't imagine the pain my mother endured after having lost so many babies. I remember Moma saying they had fostered many kids. One time she told me it had been thirty kids, though I have no way of verifying.

I do have a vague memory of two boys, named Mike and Bruce, living with them when my sister and I were first brought in the family. We even have pictures of us with them. I believe our parents had planned on adopting them because they had lived together for a long time. However, the boys' parents wanted them back. Losing them impacted my parents deeply. The pain of so many miscarriages, along with losing Mike and Bruce, must have been unbearable.

Little by little, my mother developed mental health issues. She struggled for years when it came to dealing with life, even after I had become an adult. Slowly, she retreated into a world of paranoia and bitterness.

My sister and I were adopted in June of 1960. I don't recall much about my life during that time, though I do have a collection of random memories. I remember getting into trouble in kindergarten and having to sit in the coat closet. I remember the horses that Dad would train, our grandparents visiting, and my mom buying a wok to cook Japanese food. Moma and Dad didn't go out often, always claiming there was too much to be done on the farm. They would go to horse shows sometimes, but I don't remember them ever going out to dinner together or to see a movie.

*Fairy tales are more
than true; not because they
tell us that dragons exist,
but because they tell us that
dragons can be beaten.*

G. K. CHESTERSON

LIFE ON THE FARM

*Be gracious to me, O God, be gracious
to me, for my soul takes refuge in You;
and in the shadow of Your wings I will
take refuge until destruction passes by.
I will cry to God Most High, to God
who accomplishes all things for me.*

PSALM 57:1–2

In the summer of 1964, our family moved about twenty minutes north to Snohomish. We bought thirty-five acres in a small valley, with three thousand feet of riverfront property along the Pilchuck River. The house was a converted barn, or at least my mother thought so. Built much like a chicken coop, it was long and narrow with tile floors glued directly onto concrete. One could stand at the front door, and look down a long hallway all the way through to the back door. There was a huge stone fireplace encompassing a large part of the living area. There were windows, but only on one side of the house, which I think bothered my mother because she often remarked about it. There were no closets, several walls had exposed insulation, and the roof had issues. Most of these things remained unchanged for the next forty years.

My mother never allowed us to have friends over to visit. I think she was ashamed of our house, though I never heard her say it. The bedroom Lisa and I shared only had paneling on two sides. The other two sides just showed the foil from the insulation. As we got older, we put up posters to cover the insulation. There was a metal pipe that stretched across the entire width of our room, and we used that pipe to hang up our clothes.

I actually loved the old house—so big and roomy.

I never heard my mother complain about the move, though it must have been a difficult transition. She was a city girl, born in Spokane but living most of her young life in Seattle, and had probably never envisioned herself living on a farm. But she was a trooper and went about the business of setting up her home. She placed her lovely china on a maple hutch and her bright-colored linens on the kitchen table.

The following summer, our grandparents, Anna Mae and Archie (her second husband) moved to the property. My sister and I loved going to their house. We would fish and take long walks with Pop, our special name for Grandpa Archie. I remember catching my first fish at the lake house. Sometimes during the summer, Lisa and I went on vacation with our grandparents. My parents never went. Sometimes our grandparents took us to Cama Beach on Camano Island, but usually we visited Eastern Washington. We would stay at Campbell's Resort in Chelan or go to Thorson's on Soap Lake.

The summers in Soap Lake awakened a curiosity in me because I was told that was where I was born. Lisa was born in the town of Moses Lake about ten miles away. Our grandparents never told us why we went to Soap Lake, and I suppose I will never know. It is a mineral lake where people go for health reasons, a town of about two thousand, and usually about 105 degrees in the summer. We had an unusual sense of freedom in exploring the little town together. The resort had shuffle board, and there were paddle bikes to use on the lake down the shore a bit. It was a shallow lake with sticky mud on the bottom, and you had to walk way out to swim. Best of all, there were usually a couple of other kids there, and Grandma and Pop let us hang out with friends during the day. We never had this freedom at home, and I loved it. It didn't matter that it was not the ideal place.

Having our grandparents living next door was fun and a blessing for all of us. Every day after school, my sister and I would walk down the long driveway from the bus stop and head straight to Grandma and Pop's house before going home. It was good for mom to have her mother close by. Grandma Anna Mae had always been a source of strength for our family. Grandma had a quick wit and loved to dress in classy clothes. She loved doing needlework, sewing us clothes, and wearing pretty jewelry. She was the one who taught Lisa and me how to do many things. Our mother also taught us things, but seemed more distracted by life.

While things were never easy, we had some good times during those years. Though my dad's life revolved around horses and working with machinery during the early years of my life, he actually designed the pins that hold up the Space Needle while it was being built for the 1962 World Fair. Some have doubted that fact, but my sister found the patent letter for an "anchor device" that proves the story.

Dad also had a real estate license, but ended up spending most of his time helping friends fix equipment, or battling with the county over issues with our three thousand feet of riverfront property. My father had a magnetic personality that drew people to him. He was a man with a cause and passion, but his passion seldom made money. Sometimes he would have several projects going at once. Other times he did not have work, and there was no income.

We spent our summers haying fields and swimming in the Pilchuck River. There was a subdivision on the other side of the river, and kids from there would often swim with us, hunt crawdads, and play in the sand. These were some of my favorite times.

I look back on our lives and see that we were country kids

being raised by older parents. We never discussed amongst ourselves how we felt about things. The old phrase "children are to be seen and not heard" was the philosophy in our home, so we kept things to ourselves. I remember a time when Lisa found a piece of paper that had our birth names on it. We were nine and eleven then, and it was the beginning of years of wondering. Though I don't remember ever being told, I had always known we were adopted. I didn't want to hurt my mother's feelings, so like everything else, we never talked about it.

Moma had experienced a lot of pain in her life, and she struggled with it so much that it affected her mentally. She often felt we were against her and would tell us that we were mean to her. Sometimes she would tell us that if we didn't like it there, we could go back to where we came from. This hurt me deeply, but I usually would not let it show. Once, when I was a teenager, she said it, and I grabbed my Bible and walked three miles to a friend's house. I wanted her to see the hurt her words caused me. Somehow my sister found me and took me back home. Running away had not been the right thing to do, but I needed someone to know my hurt and to see my pain. I realize that my mother may have not meant what she said, but it caused me intense pain and I wanted to be free of it.

I think Moma was unhappy living on the farm. She had no friends, or at least none that we ever saw. She fell into a deep depression and drinking. My father drank too, but he seemed to be better equipped to deal with life. He would get up early, go fishing, read a book, and have a hot breakfast ready for us by the time we got up. We never actually saw Moma in the mornings.

I recall times when Dad would tell us that everything would be okay. Looking back, I know that was denial. If you don't talk about it, you don't have to deal with it. Right?

One day, Moma locked us all out of the house. Dad just walked to his car, climbed in, and read the newspaper.

There are many other events that stick out from those years, most of which I would rather not remember. Even though we never interacted with other families, I somehow knew that the lives of most families were much different than ours. Surely other families encouraged each other, went on trips, and had fun together. I had never witnessed such things, but I knew it must be true.

However, it was not all bad with my family, and we had fun times too. On Saturdays my dad would watch John Wayne theatre, and he would make us shrimp cocktail or cook pork rinds. He would set up TV trays so we could watch movies together. Sometimes he and my mother would dance to Lawrence Welk, and I was thankful for those times when we could see glimpses of their love for each other.

Melody Beattie wrote a devotional on Luke 11:9 -13 in *The Recovery Bible* that describes how Lisa and I often felt.

Sometimes it takes hard work and much energy to get what we want and need. We have to go through the pains of identifying what we want, then struggle to believe that we deserve it. Then we may have to experience the disappointment of asking someone, having the person refuse us and figuring out what to do next. Sometimes getting what we want and need is not so difficult. Sometimes, all we need to do is ask. We can go to another person, or God, and ask for what we need.

But because of how difficult it can be at times to get what we want and need, we may get trapped in the mindset of believing it will always be that difficult. Sometimes, not wanting to go through the hassle, dreading the struggle, or out of fear, we may make getting what we want and need much more difficult than it needs to be.

We may get angry before we ask, anticipating the fight we'll have to endure. By the time we talk to someone about what we want, we may be so angry that we're demanding, not asking; thus our anger triggers a power play.

Or we may get so worked up that we waste

far more energy than necessary fighting with ourselves, only to find out that the other person, or God, is happy to give us what we want.

That devotional is a decent summary of what our home life was like. No one communicated, and Lisa and I pretty much gave up on our dreams without ever asking.

I could not grasp it back then, but it is clear to me now that my mother struggled with so much pain and couldn't cope with all the losses she had endured. Being a child, I could not see the plan God had for us, but I can look back now and see the bigger picture.

This was how my life began, and this is how my family lived. I never felt cheated because of the lack of material things, but I did often wish things for my family had been a bit more "normal." I was a dreamer then, and I am a dreamer now. It took me many years to finally get to the point where I could trust God's sovereignty.

PSALM 27:10 (NKJV) SAYS,

"When my father and my mother forsake me, then the LORD will take care of me."

He loves me, and He's in control. When I was a child, I was unaware of this promise, but I am thankful I can now see how He protected me through it all.

Courage is being afraid but going on anyhow.

DAN RATHER

THE DAY IT ALL CHANGED

The LORD is near to the brokenhearted, and saves those who are crushed in spirit.

PSALM 34:18

On February 3, 1972, our lives changed forever. It was a school day and a cold winter morning. Our driveway was long, so our father drove us to the bus stop in our old bronze-colored Bonneville. I remember I was walking to the car when he turned to me and said, "A word to the wise: don't eat yellow snow." He would always joke with us like that.

Later that morning, he met a game warden down by the river on our property. He ended up in an argument about some fences that had been cut. Soon after, he had to go get some hay for the horses from a neighbor's barn. However, the tractor was not working, and he got angry once again, yelling at the broken-down tractor. My father had a temper and was not shy about letting his thoughts be known. At that very moment, my mother came out of the house to bring him a cup of coffee. She saw him fall from the tractor and land on the ground. He had had a heart attack.

I was at school when it happened and remember hearing the siren. Having no idea what was transpiring at home, I joked around with my friends as we tried to guess what kind of siren it was. Was it a police car? Maybe it was a firetruck or an ambulance. When we stepped off the school bus, our grandpa was there with our car to pick us up. He had never done this before, and a warning bell went off in my head.

He looked at us with sad gray eyes and said, "Your mom has something to tell you." As we approached the house, we noticed our neighbor's car parked out front. Then, we saw our mother run from my grandparents' house to ours. Lisa and I immediately followed her inside. We walked through the door and stood before her in the middle of the living room. She looked directly at us and said in a quiet voice, "Your father has died." Her whispered words hung in the air like heavy clouds. We stared in disbelief, and then ran to our rooms.

I cannot imagine what it feels like to tell your children that their father has died. It must have been so hard for her. There were many times over the years when she reminded us that we should have comforted her that day, but we were just teenagers and in shock.

Going back to school later that week was surreal. I remember walking down the hall of the junior high school while kids lined up watching me. I went to my first period class, where my math teacher said quietly, "Please accept my condolences."

I burst into tears. My sister had similar experiences at her high school. I would not expect young people to know how to respond to a friend going through the loss of a parent, but I admit to feeling that losing my father had put me into some sort of new category.

While planning the funeral, we realized that since we no longer went to church, we did not know anyone who could conduct the ceremony for us. The funeral director recommended a young pastor in town who had officiated at many funerals and was gifted in helping people dealing with grief. He himself lost his father at a young age. Pastor Darrell would soon become an integral part of our lives.

It was my first time going to a viewing. I walked up to the casket and looked down at the body of my father. He didn't look like the man I knew, a man who had been so full of life. His cheeks were sunken in, and his skin had an ashen appearance.

The weeks following the death of my father were a blur. After the funeral, I began trying to adjust to life without him. It was all just a bad dream.

I am sure Moma was completely overwhelmed. We had

to decide what to do with thirty-one horses and how to feed them. They had been such a huge part of our life, and we all had our own horses. My favorite was my leopard Appaloosa named Buckshot. He was also half Arabian, so he had a silver mane and tail with the dished face and arched neck. He was white with reddish spots. I also had two mares, Tinkerbell and Wendy. We had no choice but to sell the horses. My heart ached, and I wanted to scream, but we had no savings or insurance policies, and we were even out of hay.

The biggest challenge of all was that my father did not have a will—nothing whatsoever that would indicate what his intentions were for his family. We did not have a support network, especially since my mother had no close friends. My parents had a friend they had known years before who also had horses, so my mother decided to contact him. She asked him to appraise each of our horses and sell them for us at auction.

Sitting at the kitchen table while he went through the list of horses, I knew he was not pricing the horses for what they were worth. I was just a young teen, so I didn't feel it was my place to say anything. Then I watched them catch the horses and load them into trailers. I was still in a state of disbelief as I stood in the doorway of the barn, crying. I wished for things to be different, and I was still in shock by all that had transpired.

Years later, we discovered that the so-called friend who had helped our mother price and sell the horses had ripped us off. A man who had purchased my father's parade horse came by the farm to meet my mother. He told us what he had paid for the horse, and the amount was higher than what we had received for *all* our horses. Yet another scar to remind me that life was not fair.

We also had guns, tools, and saddles. Many things Moma wanted to give to others, which was so generous, but now I am thinking it would have been helpful to sell them, even for a few dollars.

The fact that there was no will proved to be the worst thing. Most people don't think they will die in their fifties. My dad was full of life and had probably not even thought of making a will. Because Lisa and I were both under the age of eighteen, and there was not even a letter saying what my father's wishes were, the judge decided to divide everything equally between the three of us. The judge decided my mom would not be able to sell any of the property or make any changes to the property. This created a lot of problems. It would have been helpful to be able to sell some property to help tide us over for a couple years. We would each receive $90 per month from Social Security, but Lisa and I gave ours to Moma.

It is no wonder that when I study the Bible all these years later, verses that speak to helping people in need really stand out to me. I love this particular passage:

> *"You shall not harden your heart,*
> *nor close your hand from your poor*

brother; but you shall freely open your hand to him, and shall generously lend him sufficiently for his need in whatever he lacks. ... You shall generously give to him, and your heart shall not be grieved when you give to him, because for this thing the LORD your God will bless you in all your work and in all your undertakings. For the poor will never cease to be in the land; therefore I command you, saying, 'You shall freely open your hand to your brother, to your needy and poor in your land.'"

DEUTERONOMY 15:7B, 10–11

you make me feel happy

I've learned that people will forget what you said, people will forget what you did, but people will never forget how you made them feel.

MAYA ANGELOU

LIFE CHANGES

Give ear to my prayer, O God; and do not hide thyself from my supplication. Attend unto me, and hear me: I mourn in my complaint, and make a noise. ... And I said, Oh that I had wings like a dove! for then I would fly away, and be at rest. ... As for me, I will call upon God; and the LORD shall save me. Evening, and morning, and at noon, will I pray, and cry aloud: and he shall hear my voice. ... Cast thy burden upon the LORD, and he shall sustain thee: he shall never suffer the righteous to be moved.

PSALM 55:1–2, 6, 16–17, 22 KJV

About a month after my father's death, Pastor Darrell, the young man who had conducted the funeral, came to the farm and invited us to visit his small Baptist church. Grandma was so excited for us all to go. I think she was sad that we did not go to church any more. It was very different from the previous church we had attended. On the morning we attended, they were memorizing Romans 12:1–2 out loud as a congregation. That passage of Scripture is still a favorite of mine.

> *Therefore I urge you, brethren, by the mercies of God, to present your bodies a living and holy sacrifice, acceptable to God, which is your spiritual service of worship. And do not be conformed to this world, but be transformed by the renewing of your mind, so that you may prove what the will of God is, that which is good and acceptable and perfect.*

Everyone in the congregation had Bibles with them. Our previous church had not studied the Bible in such a meaningful way. Lisa happened to have a friend who attended that church, and they invited us to the youth group that night. We connected with the youth group and made many friends there.

By the time summer came around, both my mother and sister had spoken with Pastor Darrell about asking Jesus to be their Savior. One night we sat at the kitchen table, and they prayed wholeheartedly to make Jesus Lord of their life. I went through the motions. Later, we began baptism classes. I recall the deacons asking for Bible verses that were special to us. Lisa answered, and I wondered how she knew what to say. How had she learned and understood Bible verses so quickly?

They were baptized sometime later that summer, and I was too, but I came to realize my faith was not real. I needed to talk to God about my own relationship with Christ and make it real. One night, all alone, I did just that.

The Bible says, "Believe on the Lord Jesus Christ, and you will be saved" (Acts 16:31 NKJV). But you have to truly believe what He has done for you and be sincere in that belief. It is like a present under the Christmas tree that must be opened in order to see what is inside.

I think of this now and the times I have led someone to Christ. Are they just reciting words they memorized? Do they fully understand what and who they are committing to? I don't believe we need to know all the answers. Jesus said to come as a little child (see Matthew 18:2–4). But you need to see yourself as someone who needs God and that Him sending His Son to die for your sins and bridge that gap is the basis of the gospel. The growing and understanding takes a lifetime.

In the year that followed, we experienced several more life changes. My grandmother had leukemia, and her health was deteriorating. She told us that they would be unable to take us on a vacation that year, but they had purchased us a tent. We put that tent up every year after that, and we'd camp out all summer long.

In her final days, my grandmother grew weaker. I would often sit by her bed, and she would ask who it was that was standing at the foot of her bed. Was it an angel? A few days later, my grandmother died.

Once again, we were overcome with feelings of despair. As a new believer, I knew God would heal and give hope in times of crisis, but I felt as though there were waves pulling me under. I could not help but wonder why God allowed us to suffer. When Pastor came down to the farm that same morning, I asked him, "Why has God done this to us?"

He was just a young guy around thirty. I think now it must have been a hard question for one so young. I don't even remember his answer—not because he did not answer but because of the state I was in and the despair I was feeling.

There is an old poem by Annie Johnson Flint that expresses well what I feel in my heart, and how God's promises have pulled me through times of depression and hopelessness.

His grace is great to meet the great things—

The crashing waves that overwhelm the soul,

The roaring winds that leave us stunned and breathless,

The sudden storms beyond our life's control.

His grace is great enough to meet the small things—

The little pin-prick troubles that annoy,

The insect worries, buzzing and persistent,

The squeaking wheels that grate upon our joy.

Times were tough, and we had little money. Our father dying at the young age of fifty-eight, without a will, caused us to endure many problems. We lived in an old house that had many plumbing and electrical issues. We had baseboard heaters in our home. I would guess that over half were not working.

My sister and I even shared our clothes, though she was about seven inches taller than me. I would tape up the ends of my pant legs so I could wear them to school. Our mother was choosy about things like clothes, so even though we did not have many clothes, what we did have was of good quality.

For years, our mother was the one who cut our hair, but usually we did it ourselves. When my sister was in high school, she began going to a salon. I was amazed at what they did with her hair. Lisa is tall and lean. She has beautiful big green eyes and sable-colored hair. Her hair is straight, so she was able to have cute styles. I usually cut my own hair and wore it long. During my sophomore year in high school, I decided to try a salon for myself. The stylist layered my hair, and I loved how it looked. When I returned home, my mother told me my hair didn't look any different than when I cut it myself. It would be decades later before I ever visited a salon again.

Life for me was overwhelming, and I continued to question all that had happened to our family. I *never* again went to a stylist until after I was married and probably could count on two hands the number of times I had ever gone until I was about fifty-six years old. Then I took the plunge and decided it was not a waste to do. Years…years of feeling guilty for doing something for myself. Forty years of scar upon scar from not being allowed to savor something as soothing as a haircut. I so enjoy Mallory, my current stylist. All the women in our family go to her now. I'm so thankful for how much fun and special she makes my time out. At times I still feel a bit extravagant and question it, but I have to shake it off. It's okay.

As a new believer, I didn't know many Scripture verses, but for some reason I knew about the book of Psalms. There were several verses that I took as promises, and they offered me the only hope I could find. I could relate to King David, who would often question God when times were hard. "Be gracious to me, for my soul takes refuge … until destruction passes by. I will cry to God Most High, to God who accomplishes all things for me. He will send from heaven and save me; He reproaches him who tramples upon me. God will send forth His lovingkindness and

His truth" (Psalm 57:1–3). Being a young teen, I may not have totally grasped what I was reading, but it still gave me comfort. We don't always have to fully understand God's Word to feel His comfort.

In those days we had three dogs and around twenty-five cats. Our house smelled of cats, and I'm sure my mother was depressed and did not know what to do about everything. Lisa and I had to figure out what to do with the cats. We couldn't afford to take care of them, and they were destroying our home. Moma let us make the decision to get rid of the cats. She never questioned where they went. But she knew they were gone.

Sometimes I am still amazed that we were not permanently scarred by these events in life that the average young person could not even imagine. There was no one around to help us figure out life, so we did what needed to be done, and we did that every day. I believe wholeheartedly that God protected my sister and me during those years. He was honing us and molding us to be caring young women.

Another psalm that speaks to my heart is Psalm 72:12–13: "For he will deliver the needy when he cries for help, the afflicted also, and him who has no helper. He will have compassion on the poor and needy, and the lives of the needy he will save."

There were many times when I felt as though I was all alone, and that we were in a hopeless situation—day after day, week after week, month after month. Perhaps you have gone through times like this as well. During these times, God's Word gave me hope. I would read passages and have my hope renewed and know I would find a way out. No matter how bad things became, I am thankful that I had my sister in my life. When things were at their worst, we had each other. Often, we would sing together the song "Sisters" from Bing Crosby's *White Christmas*.

In 1975, Lisa went off to college. She had originally planned to attend the local community college, but I really hoped that she could go to school farther away. I was afraid that she would remain trapped, living with a mentally unstable and alcoholic mother who never ceased to tell us that life was hopeless. The previous summer, I met a woman at church camp who was the secretary to the president of Los Angeles Baptist College. I sent her a letter and told her of our situation. Within two weeks, Lisa got a letter with an offer for a work-study job and plan for her to attend. She left two weeks later. I was so happy for her to be free of our home. I wished the same for myself and knew that I would eventually be free.

Please understand that we dearly loved our mother, but years of her telling us how terrible we were, and that we should go back to our real mother, took a tremendous toll on us. Life had worn her down. She had been depressed for years. She told us for years how we were terrible to her, and that we should go back to our real mom.

Looking back, I believe the most damaging times to my own mental health were the times Moma would sit us down at the table across from her and ever so quietly tell us how terrible we were. She would speak softly and pause as if to see an answer or an argument. We knew not to say anything because it could be used against us in a later discussion. So we would not respond. It would be at least a forty-five-minute talk. It was all I could do as a young teen to sit there. This was a very common occurrence, perhaps twice a month, year after year. I wanted these lectures to go away and never return. I longed for nurturing and kindness.

I love movies, and can often find things that I can connect with in my own life. In the movie *Letters to Juliet*, there is a young woman named Sophie who goes to Italy with her fiancé, but while there she forms a bond with an older woman named Claire. Claire travelled to Verona in search of her long-lost love, Lorenzo. The story touches me deeply, not because of the main plot, but the interaction between the two women.

There are three scenes that bring me to tears. The first of these scenes is in a graveyard. Claire's grandson yells at Sophie for taking them on a ridiculous journey in search of Lorenzo. He tells Sophie she doesn't understand true loss. His folks had died in an accident when he was younger, and he was raised by Claire. Claire tells her grandson that he is wrong. Sophie's mother left her when she was just a little girl. His parents had died, but her mother *chose* to leave her.

The next scene is supposed to be later that evening, and it shows Claire gently touching Sophie's cheeks and then, ever so carefully, brushing her hair. It was a soothing gesture to ease Sophie's pain.

The third scene is very brief but stirs my heart. You may not even notice it, but I did. Sophie is about to return home, and Claire hugs her good-bye. She kisses Sophie's head several times, intertwines her fingers gently through Sophie's corn silk hair, and gently wraps it around her fist. When I watch this scene, I feel a hand reaching up and squeezing my heart, because I have always had a strong desire to be loved like that.

They tell me I must bruise
The rose's leaf,
Ere I can keep and use
It's fragrance brief.
They tell me I must break
The skylark's heart,
Ere her cage song will make
The silence start.
They tell me love must bleed,
And friendship weep,
Ere in my deepest need
I touch that deep.
Must it be always so
With precious things?
Must they be bruised and go
With beaten wings?
Ah, yes! By crushing days,
By caging nights, by scar
Of thorn and stony ways,
These blessings are!

DR. JOWETT

DARKNESS AND DESPAIR

In this you greatly rejoice, even though now for a little while, if necessary, you have been distressed by various trials, so that the proof of your faith, being more precious than gold which is perishable, even though tested by fire, may be found to result in praise and glory and honor at the revelation of Jesus Christ, and though you have not seen Him, you love Him, and though you do not see Him now, but believe in Him, you greatly rejoice with joy inexpressible and full of glory, obtaining as the outcome of your faith the salvation of your souls.

1 PETER 1:6–9

believe Moma loved us, but I feel that mental illness, and alcoholism, kept her from showing it. She felt hopeless, with no clear way out. There were times, though rare, that we would catch a glimpse of the person she could be, and those times were precious. I recall her wrapping our gifts one Christmas Eve, and she was singing Christmas carols. Lisa and I were in our beds, singing along with her. It is a treasured memory.

I know that my mother loved Lisa and me, and truly wanted what was best for us. She sacrificed her own needs many times in order to meet ours. She simply did not have the mental strength to deal with the hardships of life. I believe that, somewhere along the way, she lost her coping mechanisms. She tried hard to become a better person. I don't know that much about alcoholism, but after my dad passed away, she never again took a drink. The paranoia and other qualities remained, but she was definitely trying.

She made arrangements with a lady from church, who is now a well-known artist, for me to take painting lessons. She saved up money so she could buy my paint supplies. At church she would hand a dollar to me and Lisa to put in the offering plate. I look back on those things now and can see that she had a generous spirit and what a good example that was for us.

Those are good memories, but I still felt that life could be better.

One winter, during high school, I stayed up all night with the fire going so the pipes wouldn't freeze. Our baseboard heaters had quit working and our plumbing was old, so we had to keep the water on a trickle. I was supposed to stay awake to keep an eye on things, but I fell asleep. The water stopped running. For years after that night, we only had hot water in the kitchen and cold water in the bathroom. My mother was not happy with me, and let me know it was all my fault. She reminded me often about that for the next month, but then finally let it drop. Her letting it go may seem like a small thing, but it was huge. I could see that she was beginning to realize that every difficult thing that happened was not directed specifically toward her. This is one example of how she really did try, very hard and with limited resources, to care for us.

I remember walking down the hallway, and my mom would be in her room or the kitchen talking about how terrible we were and how we did not do anything for her or love her. I truly believe she knew we were in the hallway and was saying these things so we would overhear on purpose. She did this over and over for years.

Once, when I was a senior in high school, my mother and I drove to town. We went to the post office, and I waited in the car. When she came back out to the car, she asked me who I was. All the way home she would turn, look at me, and ask who I was. When we finally got home, she asked me why I followed her into the house. For several days after that, she would not allow me to use the phone or contact anyone. It was like a scary scene from a book or movie, only this was real. No young girl should have to endure life in this way. My grandfather was scared too. He would walk over for dinner each night, and he could tell that my mother was not right.

Later that week, I was able to use my grandfather's phone to call our church. I told our interim pastor that I would not be able to make it to the youth meeting. He asked why, and I replied, "Moma is not feeling well." He said, "Physically or mentally?" It is amazing how intuitive pastors are. I didn't have to explain; he just knew.

He came down to the farm, and I was so relieved to see him. Within a few hours, he had her talking, and she snapped out of whatever it was. Our pastor called my sister's college and told them what had happened, and they told Lisa. She was beyond concerned for me, and admittedly, I was counting down the days until I would leave for college.

What is amazing is that, with all that was going on during those years, Lisa and I grew spiritually. We had friends at school and church, and we were making decent grades. We had fun times with our youth group, and even went on a couple trips out of state. Going places with the youth group was so much fun for Lisa and me. Knowing that others loved us encouraged our hearts.

There were only a handful of people in my life who knew

what was going on at home. I suspect some knew times were tough but maybe not to the full extent. I was fortunate to have friends in my life. One night, quite unexpectedly, two of my friends showed up at my house. Their names were Abby and Kathy, and they wanted to take me to the movies. I will be forever grateful for those two girls, who reached out to me at a time when I had so little.

I am also thankful for my best friend at the time, Elaine, who never questioned the weirdness of my home life and would invite me over to her house to spend the night. We would spend hours talking about our love of God. It was a wonderful time of escape, even if only for a few hours.

I was so thankful to be growing spiritually, and I clung tightly to God's promises. Moma made some changes too, and there were times of joy amid the hardships.

We had rats in the walls of our house for months. It was hard to get to sleep at night because we could hear them in the walls. They were quite large, about ten inches, nothing like what I have ever seen before or since. It was rather unbelievable, actually. Many circumstances in my life were. But I now know with confidence that we can rise above circumstances.

My favorite Bible verses during my high school years, and later in college, were Philippians 3:13–14: "Brethren, I do not regard myself as having laid hold of it yet; but one thing I do: forgetting what lies behind and reaching forward to what lies ahead, I press on toward the goal for the prize of the upward call of God in Christ Jesus." Well, the dogs would kill the rats, and Moma would beat on the wall at night with the broom. I can still remember being scared to go to bed at night. Then she wrote a note to put on the fridge that told Satan to get his demons out of our house. About a week later, we found how they were getting in, and within a week after that, we had sealed the house and gotten rid of the rats.

I remember when the movie *War Room* came out. I watched it over and over. If you have never endured serious trials in your life, or had loved ones go through hard times, then you may think the movie is a little over the top. Not me, because I have been there. I understand the intense need for prayer and how we tend to put God in a box, not realizing His strength and power. Today, I claim His promises, and even when I was a young girl, I knew in my heart that I would be okay. That doesn't mean I was never sad, or wished for things to be better, but it kept pulling me up time and time again.

I wish I had been a better source of encouragement for my mother during those tough years. I was a teenager lost in her own world, and my mother a single parent juggling bills, kids, and her own personal issues

In 1977, I graduated high school, and that meant the changes I had been waiting years and years for were about to happen. That was the same year my sister got married to a man named Sam. She met him in college, and I was so happy for her. The wedding was at our church, followed by a reception at our farm.

Men from church came and roofed our entire house for the wedding. What an amazing blessing it was to be so loved. My mother had a difficult time accepting the help, feeling as if it were charity. I remember Sam telling her that we have to let members of the body of Christ work and allow them to give to her. I was thankful for those who came to help us out. There were many times through the years when I longed for someone, anyone, to give us a hand.

After the wedding, Sam and Lisa returned to Southern California. Sam planned to continue his education, while Lisa went to work. Two weeks later I was off to college. I felt a little guilty for leaving Moma, but I was free! I felt as though a tremendous weight had been lifted from my shoulders. I flew into Burbank, and Lisa was going to pick me up.

I remember her running through the airport, calling out, "Nicki!" As we climbed into their little yellow VW Bug, she started crying. She turned around in her seat and said, "I am so glad you are here and safe."

I realized in that moment how difficult it had been for her to know I was still on the farm with our mentally unstable mother. I had been so excited for her to be free that I had not stopped to consider how concerned she had been for me.

I was about to embark on a new era of my life. Little did I know, I would still be affected by my past for many more years.

Every day is a chance to begin again. Don't focus on the failures of yesterday, start today with positive thoughts and expectations.

CATHERINE PULSIFER

A NEW BEGINNING

That the generation to come might know, even the children yet to be born, that they may arise and tell them to their children, that they should put their confidence in God, and not forget the works of God. But keep His commandments.

PSALM 78:6–8

My college years began, and I also attended Los Angeles Baptist College, which is now called The Master's University. I was ecstatic about being there. I was referred to by many as "Lisa's little sister," but I was proud of that. The college had outgrown its existing dorms, and there were students living both on and off campus. There were six of us in my room at the back of the house we were assigned to, which was right in the middle of campus.

I jumped right in and was excited to get involved in the student government. I was voted in as a freshman class officer with two other friends that year. Music was important to me, so I took a few classes and enjoyed that. I also played basketball my freshman year.

Moma sent my social security check each month, and I had an on-campus work-study job. Still, I believe that the college faculty prayed about my situation, and somehow my school bill was always paid. I truly believe that if we do what we believe God wants us to do, He will meet our needs. I have seen this over and over in my life. In the Sermon on the Mount, Jesus tells us, "Look at the birds of the air, that they do not sow, nor reap nor gather into barns, and yet your heavenly Father feeds them. Are you not worth much more than they?" (Matthew 6:26).

Slowly but surely, I began to see how my needs were being met. Repeatedly.

I started feeling a sense of guilt about being free from home, and the occasional phone calls from my mother did not help me feel any better. Frequently she would say, "I hope you are enjoying your life, Nicki." I knew she was alone and discouraged, but I felt I needed to be where I was—surrounded by people who were both mentally and emotionally strong. The first couple of years were especially bad. I wanted to see her, but I couldn't go home for more than a week at a time. I was not strong enough. My own emotional and mental state was so fragile that I just could not bear being around her for extended periods of time. I was finally around people who loved me just the way I was, and I needed to be stronger before I would be able to spend much time with my mom.

Whenever she called, I would be pulled back down into a dark place, as if I were drowning. I remember standing under a rain gutter during a rain storm and letting the water pour over me, as if it could wash away the pain of my past. One of the older girls there told me she remembered my sister going through the same thing two years earlier.

My friends would encourage me by sharing God's promises. I recall being on lower campus by myself, and a friend from the basketball team shared Psalm 30:5: "Weeping may endure for a night, but joy comes in the morning" (NKJV). Wow! Perfect timing, and so reassuring to know that each tomorrow is a new day. I would not always despair, and life would not always be hard. I needed to recognize all of my blessings. And my friend Jane shared Job 23:10: "But He knows the way I take; when He has tried me, I shall come forth as gold" (NKJV). Okay, so there *is* a purpose in all that we experience in this life.

One of the benefits of going to a Christian college was having so many loving friends encouraging me. They also admonished me when I had done something wrong, but I knew they loved me. In high school, I was very insecure and often wished my life could be over. I would take my hairbrush and rub my arms raw with it. Sometimes, I used a potato peeler on my hand. Insecurities plagued me for years, but I believe God had a plan for me, and it was wrong for me to feel so worthless. So, although I continued with depressed thoughts much of my life, I strove to claim God's love. Despite the continual negativity my mother hurled at me, I strove to understand and feel God's love. I was unsure if anyone could truly love me, but when I made it to college, I was surrounded by people who genuinely cared for me and accepted me for who I was.

During my years on campus, I had friends who were dealing with loss and grief. I wanted to reach out and help them somehow. I felt driven to help those who were hurting, and I discovered that doing so actually helped me get past some of my inner pain. That wasn't the motivation behind my desire to help, but was certainly a result of doing so. This drive to help others who feel overwhelmed by their trials is part of what has motivated me to share my story with others. There will always be things that challenge you—or cause you pain. The question is, can you find a way to work through the trials so you can experience inner peace and joy?

My first couple years at college, I hid out when it was banquet time. Our college would have a big banquet every spring and fall. It was a guy-ask-girl thing. They would go somewhere, sometimes down to L.A., and would have a band play or some other fun activity. If I was not out where a guy could see me to ask, then I would not feel sad if no one asked me. This sounds like twisted logic, but I was so scared of *not* being asked that I literally hid. I had a close friend who also did this—we just kept more to ourselves. That way we wouldn't feel rejected.

Ah, there it is again. The deep-down nitty-gritty reality of it all, though I did not yet see it for what it was. I was going through growth and discovering who I really was—not who my moma or my friends thought I was, but who I was really.

My sophomore year I worked as an athletic trainer at the gym. I also traveled with the teams. I worked too many hours and ended up sick most of the year. Through all of that, I tried to discern what I should really do with my life. At that point I was an Education major, but I thought many of my classes were boring. My favorite classes were my Bible classes, so I decided to change majors the following year to Biblical Ministries for Women.

My junior year brought much tougher classes, many new friends, and a boyfriend. In most of my upper-division classes, I only had a couple of female classmates. Many of my fellow students were young men who, though older than me, were continuing their studies. I often felt they were all more knowledgeable than me. They encouraged me in my studies and assisted me in my classes, but sometimes I still felt lost. There were ups and downs, and the more I studied, the more I realized how much I didn't know. All the while I was still trying to earn love in my relationships and with God.

The summer after my junior year, I finally felt strong enough to go home. I felt if I could keep my conversations with my mother shallow, I could survive the summer. Shallow conversations were best with mom, because anytime we began talking about anything important, she felt we were against her somehow. Being around her was like walking on thin ice, and we had to be careful.

My senior year was full of learning and challenges, most due to the increased difficulty of my major, and the heartbreak of not being with someone I cared for. I came to realize that I didn't need to wallow in uncertainty, but move on to the next phase of my life. I had to face the difficulty of deciding what I would do after graduating. Where would I go? I knew I could not return home. I just could not bear it after finally beginning to feel strong emotionally and spiritually. I also had no real plan for my future, so the following year I worked on campus as departmental secretary for the Bible department. I was surrounded by professors who cared for me and wanted what was best for me. I was having problems with my neck and back from typing tests and projects, so my department professors all chipped in and gave me the money to go see a chiropractor, and they even bought me a new desk chair. I had many mentors that year and will be forever grateful for their kindness.

I began a new dating relationship, though it was really more of a friendship in many ways. I never really felt that I measured up. The guy I was dating told me that being in a relationship would not ever be enough. Only God could fill that void, and I needed to be content in any situation and not depend on others to give me joy or fulfillment. I was upset after our conversation and drove my little red VW Bug clutch overly hard, grinding the gears on the way home to my apartment.

When I got there, I was so overwhelmed with feelings of rejection that I grabbed a bottle of aspirin and took all the tablets. Later, I called my friend and told him what I did. He and another friend drove me to the ER. I knew deep down he was right. I knew I wasn't ready for a relationship.

My grandfather died that Christmas. I could not afford to go home for the funeral, not to mention Christmas, and I was heartbroken. I was far away from home and had no means to get there.

My mother was having a difficult time too, and at the time I did not realize it. She was alone, had no income, and was responsible for everything. She was now alone on the farm for the first time in her life. What would she do with thirty acres and three thousand feet of riverfront property? I think she was allowed to go through this difficult time so she could become free of her despair and form a new outlook. She hit rock bottom.

Our pastor had moved to Idaho a few years before, and the new pastor did not recognize the needs of my widowed mother. He rarely ever checked on her. I am greatly burdened in my heart for widows.

It was a lonely time for all of us, and I needed to realize the fact that I did not need others in order to experience fulfillment in my life. Still, I did not do much better the following year. I needed to find someone to be accountable to, but instead I just did my own thing. I learned my life lessons slowly. I believe as you go through life that you often experience the same problems because it takes time for you to work through them. This can be a difficult process, certainly not pleasant, but the outcome is worth it. As you mature and grow, you will learn how to overcome struggles.

That may sound trite, but it is true. Have you ever gone through a difficult situation, maybe for the umpteenth time, and suddenly a light bulb goes off in your head and you see clearly how to resolve it? Your experiences can help others too. I have friends who have told me, years after I shared with them about a struggle I experienced, that they were helped by what I shared, that my trial helped them in their own tragedy. I began to see how I could help others with their hurts and reach out to help them. It would take years before I truly felt I could really do this, but it was a start.

Maybe you, dear reader, are gripped by pain. Maybe you, too, have someone in your life weighed down by their past feelings of hurt, rejection or grief. I firmly believe you can get past whatever has wounded you. You can move on, grow, and change or you can help those around you.

My past is too heavy for me
to bear, Lord.
It makes me weak
and ineffectual.
Thank You for
taking the burden
from me.

CORRIE TEN BOOM

GROWING UP AND NEW DISCOVERIES

For they disciplined us for a short time as seemed best to them, but He disciplines us for our good, so that we may share His holiness. All discipline for the moment seems not to be joyful, but sorrowful; yet to those who have been trained by it, afterwards it yields the peaceful fruit of righteousness. Therefore, strengthen the hands that are weak and the knees that are feeble, and make straight paths for your feet, so that the limb which is lame may not be put out of joint, but rather be healed.

HEBREWS 12:10–13

After graduating, I moved into an apartment near the college with a couple of dear friends. We had a lot of good times together. I attended a local church but had no real accountability and, truthfully, was not living the life I should. I was just living for myself with no real direction. I wasn't even seeking direction. Deep inside I had a desire to love God and serve Him, but outwardly I wasn't sure what I wanted.

Most of my friends had made plans for their future, but all I wanted was to remain in the haven I had created, eat quesadillas, and hang out with the few friends I still had in the area. I was definitely a free spirit. I did not grow up in a home where there was a healthy structure. I paid my bills but had no clue about saving money, not that I had extra. I went to church occasionally, but did not have any close friends there so I would not connect with anyone there during the week.

I spent far too much alone time, which is not healthy for a person with a tendency toward melancholy. I would sit around and think about every mistake I ever made, every wrong word, and every sin. I still had a desire to help others, but how could I do that with the state of mind I was in?

I never wanted to be a stereotypical leader in whatever ministry I took part in. I also did not want to follow traditional guidelines for working within the church. My term paper two years before was entitled "Jesus as a Revolutionary."

Jesus reached out to the hurting, and he also showed the significance of women and who they could become. I wanted to make a difference in people's lives too.

As I look back now on my zeal and passion as a newer believer, I was a little like the disciple Peter. I threw myself into everything without thinking. I still find myself doing this. I see what needs to be done, and I desire to help whoever needs help by whatever means necessary. Sometimes it is better to think through a plan, but I am slow to learn.

Something that helped me was writing letters to God. I bought a single-subject spiral notebook and wrote down all of my thoughts. I figured if King David could do it, I could too. I told God I felt alone. I told Him I felt hurt. I told Him no one loved me—*really* loved me. I wrote pages every night. The thing good about doing this rather than just praying is that you think longer on what you are writing. It helps you connect.

My roommates during the years I was living in the apartment had all come from loving Christian families. They had a solid support network. I truly envied this aspect of their lives. I had no real guidance, and no one to call when I was hurting or when I needed advice. Although I had been adopted, and was not technically an orphan, I still felt like an orphan in many ways.

I am not making excuses for sin and for not honoring God. Sometimes I knew that I had holes in my heart that never quite healed. I led a busy life as a twenty-three-year-old, but I was not reading the Word as much as I should. I believe that having other Christians around and reading His Word helps us stay true to what is right. We really are who our friends are, and I think sometimes we ignore the signs that we are straying away from God. I was getting desensitized and allowing bad things to overcome me.

Sometimes we deny His grace and mercy in our lives. We don't fully understand grace is free, and we just need to humbly come before God and truly believe He has our back. No matter what sin, no matter who rejects us, no matter how low we become—He wants to love us. He wants to be merciful to us. He wants to show us the way out of our bad situations. I am thankful for the helpful friends I had, but I was on a rocky road and did not allow them to help. This was nonsensical. I truly wish I had allowed people in my life to help me through this difficult time.

The following year after working on campus, I began working part time in a restaurant at Six Flags Magic Mountain. I was trying to bring in some extra income. Working at the college did not pay enough for me to pay rent *and* pay off my student debt. I had heard that someone was coming home from college, his name was Craig, and he would soon be working there managing the kitchen.

I started at the restaurant and Craig, who was five years younger than me, started soon after. He had worked there previous summers, and everyone knew him. Then he came, just a young guy with big soulful aqua eyes. There were several of us at the restaurant, including Craig, who would go out together after work. Craig and I would talk for hours, even when we had to open the next morning. I discovered a very sensitive young man whom I appreciated greatly. At the time I don't think I considered a serious relationship with him.

One afternoon after work, we went to the movies with one of my roommates. When we got back to my apartment, there was a group of twentysomethings in my hot tub. They were friends and would occasionally drop by to have dinner, sing, and pray together. They had let themselves in, or maybe they hopped over the fence. I told Craig he could stay and that we would likely have a worship time of some sort.

He wanted to stay and did so until he had to leave two hours later because he opened the next day at the restaurant. I walked him out to his car, and he turned to me and said, "Wow! I haven't been to anything like that before. I got saved at a youth retreat several years ago, but have not really grown much."

I do *not* recommend anyone doing this, but I took Craig's statement that he was a Christian to mean that it was the perfect scenario for me to pursue a relationship with him. I did not think it through or consider any other course of action.

Craig had an amazing family. His dad was a structural engineer and his mom taught adaptive PE for L.A. city schools. He had grandparents, aunts, and a younger brother.

This was more people than I had ever had in my family, and I enjoyed them immensely.

We spent the following year a considerable distance apart. He was in San Luis Obispo, and I was living in Santa Clarita. We got engaged the following summer and were married in December. I am thankful for the life we have, and I am amazed at the man he has become through God's grace. However, I still do not advise anyone to rush into a relationship just because you think it "may" work out.

While Craig was in San Luis Obispo, Sam, Lisa, and I took a trip to my mother's farm. We arrived to find things in a mess. There were people renting my grandparents' old trailer, but they hadn't paid rent in three months. The many acres of blackberries were overgrown, and people were partying on the beach near the main swimming hole and leaving dirty diapers and broken beer bottles. It was clear that our mother could not handle all those issues on her own. Sam decided that he and Lisa would move from their home in Woodland, California, to Snohomish. They evicted the delinquent renters and moved within a month.

It was hard for Lisa to leave her cute little home in California and the church they had grown to love for six years. They left their friends behind too. Sam, who had plans to be in church leadership, walked away from being mentored by a wonderful man. It was a significant sacrifice to move to the farm and take care of our mom. I could not do it. I love them for the wonderful thing they did—giving up years of their lives to love and support our mother.

This now became a new era, a time when Moma had loved ones near her once again. There would be many adjustments to make, but Moma was happy to have them there. Not that there would not be adjustments, but she was no longer alone, and as grandbabies came, she would have a new joy to fill her heart.

The son of a psychologist, Sam was amazing when it came to talking with people. I think he felt he would be able to help Moma get past some of her paranoia and other issues, but after a few years living there, he concluded that keeping things shallow and loving her were the best things to do. He continued to help her until her death almost thirty years later.

After Craig and I got married, we lived for a year and a half in San Luis Obispo so he could finish his computer science degree at Cal Poly. We lived in a 350-square-foot duplex near the campus, which was great since we only had one car. Craig walked to classes, and I worked during the day. Craig was also assistant manager at Taco Bell, usually working nights and weekends. Our small duplex did not have a dining area, so for some time we would sit on cushions on the floor since we did not have a sofa. We had a huge desk, and Craig had his computer to do homework. We eventually found an old olive-green sofa that would become our sofa for the next five years. It wasn't much to look at, but it was better than sitting on the floor.

We found a great church in San Luis Obispo where we attended a young married couples Sunday school class aptly named the Gold Band Class. Many of the young adults in the class were also attending the university. Those people became friends and a solid influence in my life. I am still close friends with many of them. They were friends that were not afraid to encourage or admonish, and they cared deeply for me and Craig.

I worked two jobs: one for a brief time at JC Penney, and then the remainder of the time, I worked in the new accounts department of a credit union. I appreciated having new mentors in my life who taught me about working hard and to not always expect a pat on the back. I learned not to be concerned with how others performed their jobs and to focus on doing a good job myself. At home, I continued doing art and crafts and was thankful that Craig put up with my art mess and was always supportive.

In 1986, Craig graduated with a degree in Computer Science. I knew he would get hired by a good company. Craig is a hardworking and extremely bright man. I asked him once not long after we were married, "Isn't it finals week? Why aren't you studying?" He responded, "If I do my homework, then I don't need to study because I have learned what I need to know." That was a way of thinking I was not familiar with, because when I was in school, I had to study for all my tests.

We moved to San Jose, where all good software graduates went at the time. I said for Craig to find a job anywhere but the Bay Area. We lived there for five years and had our first three kids there: Jessica, Emily, and Nathan. I had our first child, Jessica, about four months after we moved. We moved into a 700-square-foot triplex with a garage and a small yard. I was so excited to have a garage, and Craig could have a little workbench. The yard had a small shed out back in our little grassy area. Our landlord kept a mower there and whoever lived in our part of the triplex got to mow the front yard of the triplex and receive a discount on their rent.

I was glad to have had such a great church. I found some amazing friends there and spent time each week with many of them.

Craig was a software design engineer for Hewlett-Packard. Although we had a great church home, and many wonderful friends, we knew we couldn't afford to buy a home there, so we began the process of looking for a new place to live. I thought we would be able to relocate in Washington since that is where I had grown up. Craig interviewed and looked for opportunities in that area for more than a year. I was anxious to move but realized life still went on. Sometimes you have to be silent and trust God, and that is when things happen.

Meanwhile in Washington, my birth brother, Don, called my moma. He had found out from my birth mom, accidentally, that he had two sisters. He was furious no one had told him or Larry, our other brother, about Lisa or me. Moma told Lisa, who had recently moved onto the farm. Lisa was unsure and called me. Think about what a startling thing this would be. I mean, we already had a family, and there was also that feeling of rejection. Well, Don and our other brother, Larry, ignored that and showed up at the farm to see Lisa. They spent time getting to know each other, and so began the years of puzzle pieces coming together.

There are still questions and pieces of the puzzle that are missing, and it was the start of something I wasn't sure I wanted. I wasn't sure if I wanted to add more family members to my life, especially family members I didn't know. The more I thought about it, the more I came to realize that our brothers had not had any control over how things had transpired. They had no control over having been separated from us. In the end, I was happy to have more relatives.

A year or so after we moved to San Jose, I met Larry for the first time. Later, I would meet his wife and children, as well as Don and his family. Lisa and I are half sisters; we were adopted together but had different birth fathers. Don and Larry, her full brothers, had partly lived with their dad growing up. Don had been in foster care for several years, and our birth mother, Winnie, never told Don Sr. about Lisa. Larry felt bad that they all knew their dad and I did not, so he researched mine, and I got a call one day to meet my birth father.

Craig continued interviewing for different jobs so we could move. He got an interview in Boise, Idaho. I wondered, "What is in Boise, Idaho?" I had never been there. I decided to go check out the place while Craig interviewed.

My former pastor Darrell and family were there, and I could catch up on things with them. Craig did not get the job but received an offer from another place. We had such a feeling of peace about Boise, and not about the other offer, so he turned it down and we waited.

Six months later he had another offer from a place we were not interested in, and he again turned down the offer. Five days later he was called about an opening in Boise. A month later we moved to Idaho and knew that was where we belonged. I wondered why we did not get the first offer. Why six months later? What happened in that six months to keep us in San Jose? I had our third child, Nathan. Jessica was four, Emily was two, and now we had a baby to move.

Around the same time that all of that was going on, our pastor at our church in San Jose died. He was diagnosed with melanoma and died within a month of finding out. Before he died, he wanted to talk to each person in our church so he could share the gospel and pray with them. He had the deacons schedule people around the clock, and when he was too weak, they would read from his Bible. He wanted to see everyone, including children and the elderly. He preached his last sermon from a wheelchair, speaking quietly due to his weakness. He was a true man of God who loved people and wanted others to have eternity in glory.

After we moved to Boise, we decided we would visit my birth father, Frank, who lived in Spokane. The meeting was more to please Larry than from a desire to meet my birth father. I felt awkward and truly did not want to meet him. As far as I was concerned, Samuel Maynard was my father. Why meet someone else? This may not make sense to someone who was not adopted, but I always felt the family who adopted me was my real family. They are the ones who wanted me. I experienced life with them, with all of its ups and downs, hurts with them, and joys with them.

We journeyed to Spokane, kids and all. And then I discovered why I was the only one who was not tall because Frank was at the most five feet eight. My brothers were maybe six four, and Lisa was about five eleven. It was an interesting discussion. It was short, and I did not talk about anything very important. I have a hard time in these types of situations. I feel awkward and unable to talk about anything relevant.

The night we got to Spokane, we met with a half sister. My birth dad had married her mother many years before. I don't recall much from the short conversation, but it was interesting to meet another relative. The following morning, we went to a convalescent hospital and met my birth father. He was in poor health and our time was short. I learned that he and my birth mother never did marry. He remembered all four of us playing together when we were very young. He told me that he did not want us all to be split up. We were all a year apart, so very close in age. We spent the afternoon with him then drove seven hours back to Boise.

I received a call about six months later from someone I did not know, who informed me that he had died. I never

really got to know him, but I never had the desire to do so. I felt bad that I did not have more feelings about him, but I had only spoken to him for a few minutes. I am thankful that I was able to meet him. I look back on this now and am not sure I would handle it the same way now. I allowed my feelings of not wanting to be there to get in the way of my asking him more questions and getting to know him a little more. He was in very poor health when I met him, and I would not have been able to stay much longer.

Sometimes we only get one chance at something—to have an impact, to learn—and then that moment is gone. Growing older, I now want to be more purposeful when talking to others. I want them to know I am listening and that I care. This does not come easy to me, and I often feel uncomfortable in a crowd of people. Still, I want to push through my fear and make a real connection with people I meet.

*There are times
when God asks nothing of
His children except silence,
patience, and tears.*

CHARLES SEYMOUR SPURGEON

STILL PRETENDING

Let the word of Christ richly dwell within you, with all wisdom teaching and admonishing one another with psalms and hymns and spiritual songs, singing with thankfulness in your hearts to God. Whatever you do in word or deed, do all in the name of the Lord Jesus, giving thanks through Him to God the Father.

COLOSSIANS 3:16–17

*D*o you ever feel like life trudges on, no matter what? Too often we go through the motions of life: school, relationships, marriage, kids, and work.

Once I was at a ladies' retreat where the speaker talked

about the different stages of life. The speaker said that the thirties were statistically a decade of discontentment. How could this be? It did not make sense to me. I mean, you have finally "arrived" at your destination, your "dream," but I think that is the problem. You arrive, but is it really your dream?

I had a picture in my head of what I thought my life should be, but there I was, a young mother going through the motions. I had a great husband and awesome kids. We had moved into a gorgeous new home in a good neighborhood. Life was busy. We were involved with helping at school and church. We loved our family and friends. We had just discovered that we would be expecting our fourth child. I loved my family deeply, but I still longed for love and acceptance in a deeper way. I would still experience waves of sadness, and I was not sure why. I denied to myself that it had anything to do with my childhood. I thought that I should simply remain faithful and do what I thought God wanted me to do.

Remember Pastor Darrell from my dad's funeral? Well, he and his family had moved to Boise years earlier, and he was pastor of a church in Boise. It felt like it was the right place for us. But something was missing. I thought that everyone should be happy and joyful all the time. I had this vision of what I thought life was supposed to be, and it was not that way. I thought Craig and I should never argue, and I should have an easy time with my kids. It is so easy to pick and choose what to be thankful for and what to fret over. I am the kind of person who thinks things need to be fair, but who are we to decide what is fair?

Studying Job in the Bible, with all his many trials, has made me realize that life is full of trials, joys, and blessings. It continues on, and you can choose how to live it. Will you choose to grow through adversity, or will you retreat to a safe haven and refuse to change? Will you choose to blame others, or will you move past the hurt and utilize it to the fullest in order to give God the glory?

Job argues with his friends through thirty-seven chapters. His friends tell him over and over to repent. They are convinced that Job has sinned, which caused such terrible things to happen to him. Job repeatedly responds that he is blameless and righteous. Job becomes more and more adamant that he is without any fault. In chapter 38, God speaks to Job and unleashes lists of powerful things that only God can do and Job cannot. Then Job answers God, "Behold, I am insignificant; what can I reply to you? I lay my hand on my mouth. Once I have spoken, and I will not answer; even twice, and I will add no more" (Job 40:4–5).

God continues to speak of His power, and then Job says, "I know that you can do all things, and that no purpose of yours can be thwarted. 'Who is this that hides counsel without knowledge?' Therefore I have declared that which I did not understand, things too wonderful for me, which I did not know" (42:2–3). God never does give the reason for all of Job's trials. He doesn't need to because He is God. He is all-powerful and He can do as He wants.

The testing and trials continued for our family. Our oldest child, Jessica, began wetting her bed a lot. She was five years old at the time. I called my pediatrician, and he said to keep a chart of every time she went to the bathroom and every time she took a drink. He said that she could be exhibiting signs of diabetes. Even when she was at school, she went to the bathroom about fourteen times a day. I decided to take her to the doctor. After they had performed a urine test, the doctor walked out to the waiting room and said, "I want you to go directly to the hospital and get a blood test, then return here with Craig."

Jessica was watching me closely, so I tried not to respond in a way that would frighten her, but I knew what was about to happen. Craig and I returned that evening and listened to the doctor explain all about pancreases, insulin, blood tests, and shots. Then we went to the pharmacy and got a meter, insulin, syringes, and lancets. We got home, and I went to my friend Cynthia's house, who is also a diabetic, and she showed me how to use everything. The doctor had explained it, but we were in shock at the time and I needed to hear it again. That night before bed, Craig said, "Our lives have changed forever."

The next morning was like something you would see in a movie. We had to all but hold Jessica down so we could prick her finger for the blood test, and then give her a shot. I mean ... a shot. I had rarely ever received a shot myself, let alone given one to my child! We were all in tears. She was trying to back away from us while Craig held her and I gave her the shot. Then I had to go to school and show her teacher and the office staff how to use a blood glucose meter. Her teacher was great and actually did a blood test on herself. Jessica was the only diabetic in the school at the time, and the school nurse had much experience with diabetics.

Life became a juggling act of trying to balance Jessica's blood sugar and trying to let her be a "normal" kid. Type 1 diabetes is not an exact science. A plus B does not equal C. Yes, it is true that you are balancing what you eat with exercise and insulin, but the weather, sickness, and stress all play into the equation. Sometimes, when our other kids would get sick, Jessica's numbers went up even though she was not sick herself.

After a couple years of dealing with everything, we were exhausted. There were times we would find her yelling, or slurring her words. She would start crashing, and we would try to get her to drink something, but instead she would chew the straw. It was almost as if she was drunk. Sometimes it would take multiple people to hold her down. It brought tears to my eyes thinking of how unfair it was for a little girl to have such a burden.

Our pediatrician told us something I will never forget. "This is where your faith comes in. Jessica's diabetes is a dripping faucet that will never go away. What are you going to do every day to take a break from it?" He was not referring to taking a break from tests and shots; there is no break from that. He was referring to me and Craig taking our minds off of it—finding a way to deal with life the way it was.

I am thankful for a Christian pediatrician who could walk this path with us. I realized I had been working hard at trying to make our lives normal, but how things were was normal for *us*. I mean, what *is* normal anyway? It all seemed so unfair, and there are times when I still think that. But Jessica was such a trooper. She would see another child in a wheelchair and say, "At least I am not in a wheelchair." Or she would say, "When I go to heaven, I will not have diabetes anymore."

About two years after she was diagnosed, we had an especially hard few weeks. We were up every night, and our emotions were raw. On Easter Sunday I was with our choir, praying before our concert. We were singing the old cantata *Written in Red*. The song at the end of the cantata, "No More Night," became stuck in my head. Tears streamed down my cheeks as we prayed. I knew one day Jessica would not have diabetes and would have a perfect body free of any pain.

God does not promise a perfect life. He does not promise a perfect spouse, children, health, or family. I was still telling myself in those days that my past did not affect who I was. I was determined to not let past family struggles, and the fact that I was adopted, keep me from being who I thought I was supposed to be. I was in a battle with myself. On one hand I was trying to do what was right, and on the other hand I questioned why things happened. Outwardly, it seemed like I had my act together, but God knew otherwise.

> *For the word of God is living and active and sharper than any two-edged sword, and piercing as far as the division of soul and spirit, of both joints and marrow, and able to judge the thoughts and intentions of the heart. And there is no creature hidden from His sight, but all things are open and laid bare to the eyes of Him with whom we have to do.*
>
> **HEBREWS 4:12–13**

Nothing is hidden from Him. It's all laid bare.

I definitely had a vision of what I thought my life should be. I loved playing with my kids and working on my artwork. I love to create with my hands. I worked constantly in my dining room on projects. I kept busy, and the kids were growing up. They saw glimpses of discontent, and I know I was not the perfect mom.

God had been chipping away at my heart, as I allowed circumstances in my life, and people, to control my happiness. I let discouragement creep in, and for several years I craved attention even though I was surrounded by loved ones. Oh, to rest in His grace. It would come, but it would be a long process.

Craig began traveling more for work and was under a lot of stress. Sometimes he was in his own world. He was a good provider for our family and worked so hard. I appreciated that very much, but sometimes I wanted him to be more in my world. I let bitterness creep in, wishing for things to be different. I sought inner peace and freedom from the turmoil within. I never experienced a lightbulb moment, but I gradually became more peaceful, understanding that God was in control. I learned to trust Him and to rest in Him.

I had goals in mind of where I wanted to be in life. I felt frustrated that I was not doing the things I had always dreamed of doing. In college I had dreamt of being in full-time ministry. I could have served in missions or been a speaker at women's conferences. But *life happened*. Truthfully, I was not ready to be helping the people I wanted to help.

I began praying for all the things I was thankful for in my life. I began to see God working on issues I needed to work on in my life before I would be ready to accomplish bigger things. I also began realizing that some of my feelings of hurt may have, in fact, been a result of my background. I had always been in denial about its influence on me. I never agreed with people using things in their life as a reason for bad behavior.

Through intense prayer about specific areas of my life, I began to see a different world unfold. I began to see that it was not everyone's agenda to be mean to me. I admit that I still feel this way at times, but I am working on it. How

selfish of me to think only of myself and my feelings. I knew that only God has the power to help me. The same God who holds the planets in their orbits and knows every hair on my head is powerful enough to work in any situation. He is a mighty God.

Psalm 37:23–24 became a new favorite passage. "The steps of a man are established by the LORD, and He delights in his way, When He falls, he will not be hurled headlong, because the LORD is the One who holds his hand." Wow! Isn't that great? I am not going to crash when hard things happen. He is a powerful and mighty God, and I can take comfort in His care for me. For it is unending, and He can give me comfort and guidance so that when "life happens," I am able to pass through whatever trial befalls me.

The meaning of trial is not
only to test worthiness,
but to increase it;
as the oak is not only
tested by the storms,
but toughened by them.

MRS. CHARLES COWMAN

Streams in the Desert

GROWING THROUGH STRUGGLES

"For I will turn their mourning into joy and will comfort them and give them joy for their sorrow. ... 'For after I turned back, I repented'; ... For I satisfy the weary ones and refresh everyone who languishes."

JEREMIAH 31:13B, 19, 25

I really wish I had known twenty years ago what I know now. I feel that I wasted time doubting God's love for me. Instead of resting in His love for me, I sought after the wrong things. I served Him with pure motives, but I had so much garbage to work through that it hindered the fullness of joy I could have experienced. Do you feel this way too?

The process of sanctification is a lifetime of growing and

changing. It does not happen overnight. However, I wish I had embraced all God had for me and trusted in His plan. Philippians 1:6 tells us, "For I am confident of this very thing, that He who began a good work in you will perfect it until the day of Christ Jesus." I know this now, but back then I still believed I was not worthy of His love for me.

In her book *Praying God's Word*, Beth Moore writes,

> Satan is an opportunist. Would he come after you while you are down? In a heartbeat ... if he had a heart. Let's wake up from our deceptive slumber and open our eyes to the fact that Satan is the one behind every childhood victimization, every suicide, and every scandalous fall of a righteous man. The word appropriate is not in his vocabulary. He's not polite, and he doesn't give us room to grieve and wait until we're on our feet again so we can have a fair fight.

Our almighty Creator had a perfect plan for me all along. I may have chosen to ignore it, but I missed out on all the blessings He had for me.

I was in a chapel once in college when someone told me that our life is like a book. If we mess up on page 84, then we may not receive the blessing on page 367. The path has changed. That doesn't mean He won't keep working in our lives, but there are consequences.

I am not going to use my past to hold me under when the waves of doubt wash over me. I started refusing to believe that every person who hurt me was out to get me. I refused to believe that I was a wretched person because someone was unkind to me. Sometimes it is about the other person, and not about us at all. I began to see myself the way God saw me.

I have always loved Psalm 139, especially verses 13–14: "For You formed my inward parts; You wove me in my mother's womb. I will give thanks to You, for I am fearfully and wonderfully made; wonderful are Your works, and my soul knows it very well." Wow! How many times did I read these verses and not claim them as my own? I did not fully accept His love, or the love of others, because I believed myself *unworthy.* Yet *He* formed me, and *He* made me just the way I am. That is so powerful. Think about that. You are specially designed. We are His, and He does not make mistakes. We are created in His image, and we have purpose and value.

I became more positive in my relationship with Craig. I prayed for him, not for him to change, but for how I could love him if he never changed. I began confronting things that hurt. I grew up not being able to talk about anything of importance, and I wanted to be able to share more with my family. So it was time, no matter how difficult, to break out of my carefully constructed shell and work on my fear of rejection, living with ADD, and my relationship with Moma.

I also wanted to work on my relationship with my newly discovered birth family.

I received a call from Larry one night where he informed me that our birth mom, Winnie, was dying. She was living in Alaska, and Larry wanted to make me aware of the situation. I had never met Winnie, though Lisa had on several occasions. I held no grudge or negative feelings toward her. In fact, I did not have many feelings at all. Frances Maynard had adopted me and was my moma, so I had no desire to meet Winnie. But the news that she was dying had an impact on me. I went to bed that night with those relatives in Alaska heavy on my heart.

I couldn't sleep. I wondered if anyone had shared the gospel with her. I felt for Larry watching his mother die. I wished I was there. At about two in the morning, Craig came out to the family room and asked why I was still awake. I told him of my concern for Winnie and Larry. He was confused since I had never met Winnie. I had never cared enough to make an effort to meet her or share my faith with her, yet there was a deep longing in my heart. I told him I felt burdened for her and couldn't stop crying for her.

It is so easy to talk to the people we want to talk to and ignore those we don't want to talk to. I work hard to show kindness to others, not just my friends or family: the cashier at the grocery, the child who bumps into me in a store, or the retail clerk who asks me four times in two minutes if I want to open an account (I have a *really* hard time with this one).

I was reminded of these verses in Romans 10:13–15:

> *"WHOEVER WILL CALL UPON THE NAME OF THE LORD WILL BE SAVED." How then will they call on Him in whom they have not believed? How will they believe in Him whom they have not heard? And how will they hear without a preacher? How will they preach unless they are sent? Just as it is written, "HOW BEAUTIFUL ARE THE FEET OF THOSE WHO BRING GOOD NEWS OF GOOD THINGS!"*

I had not even had the faintest desire to bring glad tidings to Winnie, not even to get to know or ever meet her, and then the opportunity I had was gone. Was it a missed opportunity to show love to her? I am not really sure. Her death brought new aspects to life. On her death bed, Larry asked her, "Mom, are there any more of us?" She answered, "Yes."

This began a search for another sister. Her name was Melinda, but she went by Mel. Larry did some investigating and discovered that she was born a year after me. Larry wrote this beautiful letter to her. I love this letter. He does such an amazing job telling her about her unknown siblings, without even mentioning our names.

My Dear Sister,

Until 20 years ago, I couldn't say those words above. Until 20 years ago, I thought I only had a full brother (and three half brothers...but we're going to leave them out of this initial discussion). One day an adopted girl's adopted mother contacted a birth grandmother...one day a grandmother told a birth mother... one day a birth mother told my brother and I...and one day we met our two sisters. We have become part of each other's lives, and I can't say words that mean more to me than those.

Early this year, through some misspoken words from someone who was "at the scene" so many years ago, I became aware that there was another sister. I proceeded to gather information through a sometimes bitter process. You were denied. Then you were admitted. People who could have helped wouldn't. I chased a couple dead ends. Eventually, I gathered enough information to institute an effective search.

Perhaps we have found you. And now what?

Now I'm going to tell you some things about us, about your birth family. I'm going to tell you because I want you to know, and because this may be our only communication, ever. And knowing what I'm going to tell you, you have the opportunity to put down this letter now, without reading it, and none of us will ever know. You don't have to know.

I am well aware that I am imposing what may be a monumental burden on you. My brothers and sisters are aware that I am searching, but I didn't ask their permission or approval to do so.

Onward!

Consider for a moment that within your birth family you have 2 half brothers and 2 half sisters. Within that group, we all have the same birth mother, but 3 different birth fathers are involved: yours, one for one of the sisters, and one for 2 brothers and remaining sister. None of us were raised past the age of 4 by the birth mother. I was the only one raised by a birth father.

My brother is the oldest, I am next in line (we were both born the same year!), then the other two girls. You are the youngest. We were all born within 5 years of each other.

Your brother and I lived with Mom until he was 4 and I was 3. Then we both went to live with our dad. Brother decided that he wanted to go back to Mom (yes, he was still 4) and was sent back. Mom couldn't handle it (financially, socially, or because she was so very, very young...you were the youngest of 5 and she would have only been 22 or 23 when you were born) and he was placed into foster care. He and I remained aware of each other and had occasional opportunities to visit as we grew up. But it wasn't until we had left high school and had a few years behind us that he moved to a state where I was living at the time, and we had the chance to spend time together, that we realized that we were very, very close...in our way of thinking, in our looks (people still confuse us for each other, but I'll always be the better looking of the two), in our outlook on life. We spent several years in close proximity and forged close bonds.

Your two sisters lived with their birth mom for a couple of years and then were adopted by a couple. The couple knew the birth mom and a few other relatives and so were able to keep track of at least my grandmother over the years and eventually made contact.

Our brother has been married over 20 years and has 2 daughters. One is a sophomore in college and the other a high school senior. He is a fisherman.

I have been married 25 years and have a daughter and son. The daughter is 22 and was married two days ago. She graduated college last December. My son is 20 and a sophomore in college. I am a project manager.

Your oldest sister has been married 27 years, I think. She has 3 sons. The oldest is the same age as my son and my brother's oldest daughter...they were all 3 born within a month of each other. The middle son is a junior in high school and the youngest is 3 years behind. She is a nurse.

Your other sister has been married almost 20 years, has 4 children, 3 daughters and a son. By age: the old-

est daughter is a college freshman, then a high school junior daughter, then a high school freshman son, then a daughter a couple years behind (you'll notice I'm not real good at tracking all this).

Let me throw in a sidebar here: There is another sister as well, as our birth mother adopted one of our cousins. As a replacement for all of us? Who knows. But throughout this letter I'm referring just to the birth children of a given mother.

My father is still alive. Your sister's father has passed. I do not know your father, although I may have some clues to pursue.

Your birth mother passed away this year (June 6th) of emphysema, pneumonia and cardiac disease caused by smoking. She was 67. It did not surprise us. However, other than diseases related to smoking, on your maternal side you don't have any diseases prevalent... no big cancers or anything else to be watching out for that we are aware of.

Your maternal grandparents have both passed away.

Your sisters do not smoke. My brother and I do/did (I quit 5 weeks ago and he probably won't be far behind...we don't mimic, but we do find ourselves at the same phases in life many times).

Your sisters are sustained much more by their faith

than your brothers, and pay more attention to the welfare of their souls.

The 4 of us love each other dearly and in our own ways. We are each so very different and not...your oldest sister is Type A, your other sister is Type B. You have 2 very Type A brothers. I consider each of us "a success," whatever the heck that means...we are each doing pretty much what we want with our lives.

Okay, so if the above sounds like a pretty whacked-out lineage lineup, you're right. We're still trying to explain it all to the kids and the extended family.

As far as extended family, on your maternal side, you have 2 aunts, both of whom are still living and one of which I am very close with. Between them, they have 6 children (your maternal cousins) and those cousins have another dozen or so children between them, some of whom are now having their own children.

So much for the facts.

None of us are perfect. I personally think that we each wear our individual blemishes pretty openly, but I read people pretty well and not everyone sees the same (or judges the same). One thing you'll notice about us all...we may talk about other people occasionally, but we tend not to judge. We can celebrate our differences...without agreement...and without rancor.

Our parents weren't perfect, that's for sure. But try as I want to sometimes, I can't go back and judge them for the choices and mistakes they made when they were young. Our birth mother was 17 when she had our older brother. Dad was 18. They both made choices that they have had to live with and some were harder than others. We have all done the same to varying degrees.

For what it's worth, it occurs to me that our mom may have loved you the most. She gave you up at birth, so she never knew you at all. From what I have gathered from various sources, she was in trouble and someone in a position of influence pressured her, saying, "If you give up the baby, we'll leave you alone." It wasn't too much longer after that that she adopted a baby cousin of ours (Auntie wasn't in a position to have another baby, apparently) and successfully raised her through high school graduation. And if that wasn't a "replacement" for a lost baby, I don't know what it could have been.

Do you know why I'm doing this, Sister? Do you know why I'm writing you? I'm doing it because I love my brother, and I love the sisters that I didn't meet until I was 30 years old and I'll always regret so much not meeting sooner, and they love me, and that sibling love, I truly believe, has provided us a measure of replacement somehow for at least a portion of the pa-

rental love and sibling youth that we each missed out on. In other words, we needed each other, we found each other, and we allow each other a reserved place in our hearts.

My siblings and I discussed contacting you. We discussed the impact this knowledge would have on you. To the extent any of us hesitated, it was due to our consideration of your feelings. Because we are already building a place for you in our hearts and minds, and already we don't want to hurt our youngest sister.

Our sincerest hope and prayer is that we have found you and your family well and that you have had a wonderful and fulfilling life with people who loved you deeply, and that this letter does not hurt you. Beyond that, we hope and dream that we might be able to communicate further, and meet you someday, and that we might find common ground.

Now you get to choose, lucky one! And if you so choose, then we will never see you, but we will still know you are there and we will keep your memory. And if you choose otherwise, many new arms will surround you.

**With the greatest of love and affection,
A brother**

That following Memorial Day weekend, I flew to Homer, Alaska, for a memorial service for Winnie's niece Megan's graduation and to meet my new sister. I am so thankful she was receptive to Larry's letter. I admit I was very nervous about meeting her. Larry picked me up at the airport, and we drove to Don's house, my other brother.

I walked through the door and into a crowd of people. I could see the back of a woman with curly brown hair, and somehow I knew it was her. We found out a little later that we actually have the same father. Imagine that—a full sibling!

It was a fun weekend spending time with that family. I also got to meet another sister, Shannon. Shannon is my cousin whom Winnie adopted a few years after Lisa and I were adopted out. I wish I had spent more time with her, but I was nervous about meeting new people.

Winnie's sister, Aunt Carol, and her husband, Uncle Dave, were also there. We had met Aunt Carol and Uncle Dave a couple of years prior at my niece's wedding. I will never forget what they said to me and Lisa at that wedding. Uncle Dave leaned over and said, "We have been praying for years that you and Lisa were in a Christian family." Wow! How amazing to have someone I didn't even know praying for me for all of those years.

On a side note, meeting my redheaded aunt explained why I have a redheaded son. That was a fun thing to find out.

We stayed up late talking, and I was thankful to get to know my brother Don and his wife better. Sightseeing a little while in Alaska was great too. We went to the beach at 3:00

a.m. because it was still light out. What a wonderful time I had visiting with them and learning more family secrets. I will never know everything that transpired fifty years earlier, but I now have a yearning in my heart to learn about my past. I had reservations about going, especially because Lisa was unable to go, but I am so thankful I went.

I often wonder if this is why I am such a history- and geography-driven person. I love anything that has to do with heritage or faraway lands. My siblings and I missed out on growing up together and learning more about each other. I am beyond thankful I had the opportunity to know them as adults.

The following year, Craig and I were at the movies one evening when I received a call that my brother Larry had died suddenly of a heart attack. It was a tremendous shock. He was only fifty years old. Out of all my siblings, besides Lisa, I felt I knew Larry best. He always had a warm smile and an open heart, and was the ambassador for the family. Larry wanted so much for us to be a family and for us all to love each other. His funeral was a celebration of a man who loved his family and friends deeply, and who always spoke from his heart. I am sad that I didn't know him longer.

The joy in life is to be used for a purpose. I want to be used up when I die.

GEORGE BERNARD SHAW

REALIZATION

For You formed my inward parts; You wove me in my mother's womb. I will give thanks to You, for I am fearfully and wonderfully made; wonderful are Your works, and my soul knows it very well. My frame was not hidden from You, when I was made in secret, and skillfully wrought in the depths of the earth;

PSALM 139:13–15

I felt my life shifting from wanting things to be a certain way to trying to love and accept everyone regardless of the consequences. I have always been a person who wanted to reach out to those in need. When I was a substitute teacher, I was the person who wanted to embrace the naughty kid in class. In fact, when teachers would leave notes to me with a list of students who would cause me problems, I would mark out the names. I refused to assume that those kids would be a problem for me, and they usually weren't.

I understand that to be effective in helping others, the compassion must come from within me. I began to see that the ministry I yearned for all of those years—meeting needs, reaching out to people, loving those who are hurting—had been there all along.

Our kids were growing older. We had two in college and two in high school. Life was very busy with sports, music, school, and church. I would go back home to the farm whenever I could, usually twice a year. Craig was traveling a lot, and I kept moving along.

Every day is a blessing filled with opportunities to show love to others. And some of my favorite people to show love to were on our family farm in Washington along the Pilchuck River.

Whenever we visited the farm, our kids would get to spend time with their cousins, swimming in the river, building bon fires, jumping on the trampoline, playing games, and having picnics. The farm was another home to us. Sometimes, I would stand outside and listen to the rustle of the cottonwood trees and smell their fragrance. Back at our home in Boise, there have been times when my kids were down by the Boise River and would say, "It smells like Grandma's."

I am thankful my family had time with Moma, and she loved our visits. My kids have fond memories of visiting their grandmother. Moma swam in the river with her grandkids and looked for new additions to their rock collections, which she helped them sort and polish when they got back to the house. We took day trips to Mukilteo Beach, had lunch at Ivar's, and collected seashells and sand dollars. She loved those trips with her grandkids and admiring the treasures they would find.

The kids would play outside together all day. There were wasp stings and nettle stings, and Emily cut her foot on the trampoline spring one year. As the kids got older, the adventures changed, but Moma loved them just the same. The kids made it a point to call her, write letters and cards back and forth, and visit her when they could. She always had a plate of cookies on the table, offering them to visitors.

Two of my best friends came over from Boise to see her. My friend Susan came several times. They would talk about stitchery and needlecraft projects. I am happy that my friends were able to meet Moma and spend time with her. Another time, my friend Marsha came and spent time with Moma, allowing Lisa and me to have some sister time alone.

In her later years, my mother began to draw pictures on cards with her colored pencils. She drew flowers, trees, blossoms, deer, and birds. She sent them to everyone. She even mailed cards to my friends. Her handwriting was not easy to read, but we would always giggle at the note, or at least we laughed at what we *thought* it said. At her memorial, a friend mentioned appreciating getting a snail mail letter and how much it meant to her that Frances would take time out to make her a card even though she only lived a few miles away.

As time went by, it was amazing to see the changes in my mother. She would call each of her friends every morning to make sure they were okay. She would pray for everyone in her church directory, then start all over again when she was finished. I have tried doing this a few times, but it's not easy. People would visit her, sit by her rocking chair, and thank her for praying for them. I wanted desperately to see her for the woman she had become, but I still wrestled with seeing her as a manipulative woman. It was still difficult for me to spend time with her alone.

I envied Lisa, who had been able to grow past the hurt and see our mother for who she had become. I suppose I could see it too, but I selfishly did not want to feel that others saw her as a new person. I realize that may make me sound like a monster, but I still had years of verbal abuse clinging to my memory. I saw the sweet, loving side of her that others were seeing, but whenever I caught glimpses of the old person she used to be, I would shut out the new and old memories came flooding back. My scars had not fully healed, and the process was so slow. To be freed of so much inner pain may take a lifetime.

I have said how much I love reading the book of Psalms. Maybe it's the hope it gives, and how I can relate to so many of them. Here are some verses from Psalm 55:

Give ear to my prayer, O God; do not hide…answer me…"Oh, that I had wings like a dove! I would fly away and be at rest."…As for me, I shall call upon God, and the LORD *will* save me. Evening and morning and at noon, I will complain and murmur, and He *will* hear my voice…Cast your burden upon the LORD and He *will* sustain you. (vv. 1–2, 6, 16–17, emphasis added)

God was working on my heart, giving me new eyes. He was also working on my heart toward my husband. My relationship with Craig began growing in a new way. It wasn't easy, but I wanted to work on it. It wasn't that our relationship was bad, but neither of us were good communicators, and we needed to start learning how to be better at sharing our feelings with each other.

I began praying scriptures for my husband and my kids. I would insert my children's name into a verse. I loved Jodie Berndt's book *Praying Scriptures for Your Teenager.* I have great kids, but I still had tears streaming down my face as I pleaded with God for my kids to know and love Him with all their hearts.

There were other family issues that broke my heart, and I felt alone and unsure how so many painful things could happen. I began to feel hurt over friends, kids, and church. I was doing it again, letting circumstances rob my joy, and letting people control my innermost being. I love Isaiah 26:9, which says, "At night my soul longs for You, indeed, my spirit within me seeks You diligently."

After months, or perhaps years, of crying through the night, I knew that God had bigger plans for me. I was paralyzed by certain events with my loved ones to the point where I thought my heart would break. I had to trust in His sovereignty and realize that I was responsible for myself. No one else—not Craig, my kids, friends, or church—could give me true joy and lasting peace. God wants me to be all He has made me to be, apart from everyone else. Not because I had a great family, or nice house, and not because of service I had done for Him. My time in the Word and in prayer with small groups helped to free me from myself and see how I could love God more. It was a gradual process.

Throughout this process, time in prayer and the Word set me free. Job 23:12 says, "I have not departed from the command of His lips; I have treasured the words of His mouth more than my necessary food." That has become my goal— to yearn for the Word and for time spent with God. I can't solve others' problems; I need to work on me. A sign my moma had put on the refrigerator when I was in college reminded me of this: "No one can make me angry but myself, therefore I choose to be happy." My moma, in her nineties, was happier than she had been in her entire life.

*As God is exalted to the
right place in our lives,
a thousand problems are
solved all at once.*

A. W. TOZER

FITTING PIECES TOGETHER

"I will make all my mountains a way."

ISAIAH 49:11 KJV

am amazed at the wonderful puzzle that God creates. So many pieces, from so many places, all coming together to reveal His plan. There is the piece representing me and Lisa being adopted together, the piece about our father's death, and the piece representing all of our rejection, poverty, grief, and discovery. He continues to show me His plan, and I can now see the reasons for much of what has happened in my life. I have learned to be thankful for things I thought unbearable, because I can trust in the God who has molded me, and know there is a purpose. I may not know all of my relatives very well, but my family has expanded, and I am grateful. I still want to know the why behind things that happen, but I am not hung up on it.

There remain many unanswered questions about my past. I have become curious about things that happened that I may have wondered about earlier but did not put pieces together. For instance, when we were young, people came to fish along our river banks. Steelhead was what they were after. They asked for permission to park, then walked down to the river. One day my moma asked me to "show" someone the river. *How odd*, I thought. *Why?* Although I felt uncomfortable, I went with him. Then he pulled out a Polaroid and snapped a couple of photos of me. He handed me one. I still have that photo, in which I am clearly frowning. Who was that fisherman?

There are other questions as well. Why did Winnie never tell us about Mel? Winnie just disappeared for a year or so back when Mel was born, and no one knew where she was. Some of these things were taken to the grave with people. Every once in a while, I will learn something new, or hear a new "fact," and down the rabbit hole I go. I could easily become obsessed about it all, but I don't think that would be wise. People who grow up in a home with both birth parents may not fully comprehend, but I am content to put the puzzle pieces of my life together slowly. I will continue to push forward and to be all He has called me to be.

I have an amazing family of my own. My husband has grown so much through the years, and I am thankful for that.

I have been immensely blessed with four incredible children.

Looking back at the past twenty years, I can see God orchestrating a plan of ministry for Craig and me. We have worked in AWANA children's ministry for nearly thirty years, we have been involved with several home groups, and I have taught many Bible studies. There is always something new to learn and more ways the Lord can work on my heart.

Craig also helps with running sound at our church on Sunday mornings, and is involved with our church softball team. I have loved watching him lead our small group and teach kids at church. One of my favorite things has been my one-on-one meetings with young women: listening to their burdens and fears, encouraging them, and helping them to understand that God grants an inner joy through struggles.

God has not only given me an amazing family but also an incredible church family. I don't feel like an orphan any longer.

There are many stories about this amazing group of people that God has blessed me with, but they will have to wait for another book.

We all have family. Some of us have two. Maybe you also have an adoptive family and a birth family. Some of you have grown up in a supportive, loving home with encouragement and support. I grew up in a home where I was loved, but other more nurturing factors were not there.

I have watched the movie *Saving Mr. Banks* at least five times. It is the story of the writer of Mary Poppins, Mrs. Travers. She is so broken and haunted from her childhood that she cannot get past it even decades later. Her pain is great with vivid memories of her alcoholic father whom she dearly loved. She is not able to overcome her past.

I, too, have felt this way in life—as if there is a hole that has never been filled or a harsh word buried so deep it is forever embedded in my being.

But I have a hope that I am not sure Mrs. Travers ever had. I have God's precious book of promises—promises that deliver us from the pit. Psalm 56:8–11 grants me that special promise: "You have taken account of my wanderings; put my tears in Your bottle. Are they not in Your book? … This I know, that God is for me. In God, whose word I praise, in the LORD, whose word I praise. In God who I have put my trust, I shall not be afraid. What can man do to me?"

When I stand before God at
the end of my life, I would
hope that I would not have
a single bit of talent left and
could say, I used everything
you gave me.

ERMA BOMBECK

A NEW KIND OF GRIEF

*"And I will bring the third part
through the fire, refine them as silver is
refined, and test them as gold is tested.
They will call on My name, and I will
answer them; I will say, 'They are My
people,' and they will say, 'The LORD is
my God.'"*

ZECHARIAH 13:9

For years, whenever I left the farm after a visit, I would have that sinking feeling that it was the last time I would see my mother. It began in college and continued as the years passed. The last few years of her life, I would try to go home more frequently because I could see she was becoming increasingly frail. I am so thankful for Lisa. She is an incredible nurse, and it was amazing to watch her care for our mother. It was a blessing to have a nurse next door. Lisa sacrificed twenty years of her life to care for our mother. *Twenty years.* I felt helpless at times. Having no medical expertise, I feel out of place trying to help in even the smallest way. I would make the occasional meal or go to town with Lisa so she could have some fun time. I wanted to spend more time with our mom and felt guilty that I was nine hours away.

Moma was at peace and seemed content. She would call her friends every morning. Her friends were dying with increasing frequency, sometimes as many as three in one month, and there were times where she voiced wonder at why God didn't take her home too. Why did He still want her on earth? She didn't go anywhere, so what was her purpose? God is a mighty God and has His plan worked out well in advance. I look back at that time and see the people she ministered to and prayed for. We were the ones who needed more time with her. It wasn't for her benefit as much as it was for ours. We needed time to heal, grow, and learn. I am thankful my children were able to know her and see her sitting on her bed doing her devotions or in her rocker reading and praying.

The last year of her life, she had to go into hospice care. The people who work for hospice are amazing at what they do. I feel that even though they were not there daily, because Lisa wanted to do much of the care, it seemed a great burden was lifted off of Lisa. Typically, when someone enters hospice, they are expected to die within six months. Our mother, with Lisa's care, lived several months longer.

I visited as often as I could. In October of 2013, I went for another short visit. Moma always wanted to see me off, no matter how early in the morning it was when I left to drive home. I hated waking her, but I knew she was sincere in wanting to say good-bye. It was becoming difficult for her to get up at all. I was about to leave when Lisa had awakened our mother.

Moma got to her feet, then held my hand with both of her small, thin hands. "I love you, Nicki," she said. "You have been the joy of my life."

I stood still for a moment, not knowing what to say or think, but knew in my heart that she meant it and it was a statement she had wanted to say for years. I hugged her gently, kissed her, and went out to my car. I will never forget that morning, the feeling it left, and the transition that occurred within me. It was a transition that had been going on for twenty-five years, ever so slowly. A transition of peace and joy filling her life, and a transition of my own peace that came with the knowledge that I was loved by my mother.

About a month later, as I drove to my Bible study, Lisa called and said she had Moma on a conference call. She wanted me to talk to her. I always feel odd on those kind of calls, and sort of muddle my way through, not really knowing what to say. I told her I loved her. I'm not sure what else I said, and I'm sure the call was brief.

About fifteen minutes later, as I was setting up my Bible

study area at church, I received a text and glanced down to see who it was from. It was from Lisa and read, *Moma has gone on to be with her Lord.* I think I read it out loud.

I continued with teaching the Bible study, and later as I drove home, the tears came. I didn't realize when I had talked to Moma earlier that it would be the last time I would ever talk to her. But I would not have said anything different. She knew she was loved.

We held a memorial service a month later so we could get our family there. It was a wonderful time together, celebrating a woman who chose not to continue in bitterness but chose joy. I was thankful so many of us were able to go. The theme of the memorial was how God had watched over Moma for years, even during the hard times, and gave her love so she could share it with others. So I chose to sing the old song "His Eye Is on the Sparrow" at her memorial.

> *Why should I feel discouraged*
> *and why should the shadows come?*
>
> *Why should my heart be lonely and long*
> *for heav'n and home,*
>
> *When Jesus is my portion? My constant*
> *Friend is He:*
>
> *His eye is on the sparrow and I know*
> *He watches me.*
>
> *His eye is on the sparrow and I know*
> *He watches me.*

I sing because I'm happy,

I sing because I'm free.

For His eye is on the sparrow,

And I know He watches me.

*"Let not your heart be troubled," His
     tender word I hear,*

*And resting on his goodness, I lose my
     doubts and fears;*

*Though by the path He leadeth, but one
     step I may see;*

*His eye is on the sparrow, and I know
     He watches me;*

*His eye is on the sparrow, and I know
     He watches me.*

*Whenever I am tempted, whenever
     clouds arise,*

*When songs give place to sighing, when
     hope within me dies,*

*I draw the closer to Him, from care He
     sets me free;*

*His eye is on the sparrow, and I know
     He watches me.*

*His eye is on the sparrow, and I know
     He watches me.*

Moma was indeed a sparrow that God had watched over through extremely difficult times, leading her to a time of being overjoyed with life and with everyone around her.

We all have this choice, don't we? I am sure you have heavy burdens and heartaches, and maybe you can't see past them. It took me, my sister, and our mother years to recover, but we got past them and so can you. Moma died at the age of ninety-seven, and the last thirty years of her life were the happiest of all.

Don't give up, and don't despair. God transformed my mother and healed her pain. He can do the same for you.

This morning I heard "He Knows My Name" by Francesca Battistelli on the radio. I have heard that song dozens of times and never listened to all of the lyrics. In it she sings, "Make no mistake / He knows my name / I'm not living for applause / I'm already so adored." Wow! He adores me. What an amazing thought. Why would I seek the adoration of others when the God of all creation adores me and loves me?

My mother was on her own as a child, raised her younger brother, and was on her own again as a widow. She raised two girls with no income—and little hope by worldly standards. God's eye was indeed on the sparrow.

*The best and most beautiful
things in the world cannot
be seen or even touched—
they must be felt with the
heart.*

HELEN KELLER

DAUGHTER OF THE KING

*"And I will be a father to you, and you
shall be sons and daughters to Me,"
says the Lord Almighty.*

2 CORINTHIANS 6:18

The year 2015 got off to a rough start. In January we discovered that my brother Don was diagnosed with Stage IV cancer. He came down from Alaska for treatments and further diagnosis. He was told there were no further treatments that would improve his health, only things to make him comfortable.

Emily and I went to Washington, where family had rented a home where people could stay when they came to visit. It was close to the farm so we could easily go see everyone. Sometimes the best thing to do is just to be together and share memories. Lisa was a wonderful caregiver again, this time for her brother.

One afternoon I sat by Don's bed, listening to him share his thoughts. He said he had been a good husband and father, which was true. He could not understand why he was stricken with cancer. He was only sixty years old. Sometimes, it is difficult to know how to answer someone. No matter what comes to mind, it all seems trite or insensitive. One thing is for certain: being someone who listens is always a good thing.

A couple of weeks later, I called and shared the gospel with him. I told him that God loved him so much he sent His Son to die for him, that the Bible tells us to believe and be saved. There are no guarantees in this life. There are many things that we endure, some good and some bad. Some are the consequences of choices we have made, and some have no explanation. The bottom line is that, compared to eternity, this life is brief.

As you have read through this book, you may have wondered how I came up with the title. I had a friend tell me that most adopted people probably think they are a princess. I was not happy with that statement or that he said it to me. I wished away a lot of my life, not living in the real world, dreaming. I was adopted into a better situation than I would have had. I view my adoption as me being rescued. Wondering who I was, where I came from, and why my birth parents gave me up was not beneficial for me. All of that had only fostered unforgiveness and bitterness. It stunted my growth and hindered my ability to move on. I am not really a princess. I decided to claim something far greater.

I still deal with daily struggles like everyone else. But I can overcome them because I have an all-powerful, mighty God who is my Father. I may not have an earthly father, but I have a heavenly Father and I want to be who He wants me to be.

My story is an unusual one, and people have asked me to write it down for years.

My biggest prayer as I wrote this book was that God could use me, in some small way, to tell this redemption story and to give hope to others. I implore you to deal with your pain and whatever is holding you back. Don't hesitate, deal with it now. You can turn the page on your past, on the pain you're still holding inside. Do for others. Claim His promises.

I am praying for you. I truly am. I have been praying even before this book was published. I hope that, by reading about my life, you can see that you have a *choice*. I hope that by seeing how my sister lived her life, sacrificing for the sake of others, you will find ways to do the same. Finally, I pray that my mother's life serves as a shining example that no matter how far down you are, there is a way out.

Grace is so very freeing.

God, in His mercy, doesn't expect you to have it all together. He just expects you to trust. It seems so simple and it is. Do you want to be bitter and manipulative, or choose joy over pain and suffering so that you can bring joy to others?

I want to have an authentic faith that calls out to others, helping them become more passionate for Christ. I dearly hope you can move past your burdens and times of adversity. Do *not* let months or years go by without turning the page on your pain. You can be free of the chains that hold you down. My hope for you is that you see you are a child of the King.

AUTHOR'S NOTE

There's a process to everything in life.

No matter who you are or what you plan to do, it requires a process—of thinking, praying, and then taking action. This was certainly true for me when I sat down to write.

This book was thought about, prayed about, and then finally…bit by bit, emerged over a lifetime in the making, as God formulated a plan.

The past couple of years has been a fast-paced project to finally finish. Even now as I write this, I am reminded that I may have left something out that I am not even aware of—that is, a piece to this giant puzzle. It has burdened my heart greatly to get the facts straight, and on paper. However, I've realized that it's time to let go.

I wrote this book with God's guidance, in order to provide hope and comfort.

I pray that you have gained something from within these pages.

I have already started my next book, *It's Not about the Pie.*

This book has to do with hospitality, from a biblical view. Not hospitality in the way many in the world think of it, hosting events or parties for others, but as a fresh look at all of our lives and the various ways we can help and serve others around us.

Growing up in need in so many ways allowed me to feel a burden to reach out to others who are hurting. Hospitality is far more than just giving to give or making sure everyone's having a good time. Think of all the ways Jesus was hospitable with His giving and how it truly changed lives and generations. Hospitality isn't always about hosting a party to serve those we genuinely love. Jesus demonstrated that for us in the Bible with the man in the tombs—the most despicable, demon-ridden, twisted soul. Yet Jesus crossed over and went out of his way to reach him.

My second book will cause you to think of hospitality in an entirely new way.

How can you reach the unreachable? How can we all hear clearly, in order to serve not just those in our own homes or neighborhoods but the ones we've got to go out of our way to reach? While thought provoking, it will also be practical. Some chapters will include ways to walk out the biblical perspectives that we are commanded to follow, such as reaching out to neighbors and favorite family recipes.

It will be a fun book filled with ideas that every family can incorporate into their family plan.

STUDY QUESTIONS

CHAPTER ONE

1. What verses speak to you when you go through adversity? Where do you find refuge?

2. Read Psalm 6. David is clearly distraught and crying out to God. Does Scripture give you hope? God wants us to open up to him and be honest. David treats God like his hope and shows he trusts Him. Are you able to be completely honest with Him? Is there something that you would like to be honest about with Him right now?

3. Do you have a scene from your past that haunts you? Did you grow through it? Do you need to turn the page? What can help you move past it? Sometimes it helps to write it down to uncover the hurt that is deep inside. Write out something that you still remember from years ago.

CHAPTER TWO

1. What is one event from your early childhood that sticks out in your memory? How did that event shape or change you?

2. Read Philippians 4:11–12. Paul writes to us that he learned to be content in any situation. How have you learned to be content? What helps remind you in the middle of situations to be content?

3. I was fortunate to have my grandparents living on the same farm and be able to learn many things from them. Do you have a close relative who has taught you and made an impact on your life in a special way?

CHAPTER THREE

1. Catastrophic events, deaths, terminal illnesses, and even divorce can wound us so deeply. Why do you believe God allows these things in our lives? What in your life has wounded your heart?

2. Read Psalm 37. Pay close attention to verses 4–5 and 23–24. This psalm has become one of my very favorites because it gives us such hope that God will not allow us to go through hard times without Him holding onto us. What sticks out to you in this passage that gives you that hope? Can you share your favorite passage that has given you that same promise?

3. My moma, as a widow, often needed help. I remember wishing someone would just come by and offer to help with something. Is there someone in your life or your church who maybe needs help and just hasn't asked? Are there needs that need to be filled? How can you be proactive in helping those who need help?

CHAPTER 4

1. Scripture memorization helps us to hide God's Word in our heart. In many other cultures they may only have one Bible for an entire village or family. Memorization is so important. There may come a time when we too are not able to keep our Bibles. What are your favorite verses you have committed to memory? Why? And what are some that you are working on or hoping to memorize in the near future?

2. Read James 1:2–4, Jeremiah 29:11–13, and Psalm 118:5–6 pertaining to comfort and help.

3. What is a song, book, or movie that you can relate to in your life? What made you choose this?

CHAPTER 5

1. Escape. What gives you relief from an ongoing pain in your heart? Maybe it is being out in nature, a bubble bath, or watching your favorite movie. We all need to find ways to get past an ongoing trial. I find comfort in being outside and reading Scripture, especially Psalms. God is not a God of confusion or chaos. He gives you peace. List something you can do today to give you rest.

2. In writing these study questions, this is the last one I wrote. This is kind of a dark chapter, and I really wanted to choose verses that would grant hope in the midst of darkness and despair—whatever that is for you— whether it is mental illness, addiction, grief, or other personal struggles. Please read Job 23:10–12, Zechariah 13:9, and Micah 6:8 and explain how these can offer hope to you and others.

3. Sometimes there are things or people in our lives who are unlovely—those with mental illness, addiction, loss of income, etc. We need to have compassion and love for them. What are some practical ways you can do this?

CHAPTER 6

1. Write a short letter to God. If you have something burdening you, just open up to Him. David often did this. I think that is why we all connect so much to Psalms. You may also write a praise letter.

2. We all have friends who encourage us. Sometimes we cannot even cope with a tragedy, but we have a friend or Bible study group that we know is upholding us in prayer. This is so essential to our growth because we will always remember those who have shared love with us, and then when others are hurting, we are better equipped to help them. Share about someone who helped you in your time of heartache.

3. Sometimes we stay in denial about tragedy in our life. We leave it covered up and hang on to it. It can hinder our relationships with others and with God. It is so easy to build that brick wall and pretend something did not happen. I know from my own life that it only hinders our joy. Pray for something you feel is unresolved between you and God or you and a friend.

CHAPTER 7

1. Read all of Psalm 33. How does this psalm give us hope?

2. Life is not just survival. Sometimes, however, we have heartache that may never leave us on this earth. We need to find a way to cope. Maybe it is a chronic or terminal illness, a love one who has rejected you, or something you have done that has altered your goals in some way. I have things in life and people that bring tears to my eyes. We can forgive if that is the issue, but sometimes we still may remember a scene that causes pain. Or perhaps we miss someone terribly. God promises to grant us peace, but we need to share our burdens with Him. He already knows, but still offer it up. Pray for your "dripping faucet"—the thing that may never go away.

3. Family, friends, and churches can be a good support system. Who are some people that are a part of your support

CHAPTER 8

1. Satan is a deceiver. He wants you to feel defeated. But you, dear friend, are created by God for wonderful things. What gives you confidence in how God created you? Read Psalm 139.

2. Look at Ephesians 1:3–9 and Colossians 1:13–14. How do these give you hope?

3. God wants us to share His story of salvation with others. Sharing your testimony of how you came to know Christ as your Savior is a great way to begin sharing the gospel with someone. Writing it out is a way to help solidify your personal story. Write your testimony, including verses you would share with someone.

CHAPTER 9

1. The more hurts in life we deal with, the more gets revealed to us. Some things are down way deep inside. This is part of the sanctification process, the chipping away within us and allowing God to fill those empty spaces. Write how you have seen this in your life.

2. Read Psalm 139. What are your favorite parts that you can relate to?

3. Send a "snail mail" encouragement note to someone today. I guarantee it will put an immediate smile on someone's face. Make a list of at least five people you could mail a note to in the next two weeks.

CHAPTER 10

1. Share a special family memory or special place your family loves.

2. Read 2 Corinthians 5:17. How have you become a new creation?

3. Joy is a choice. How do *you* choose joy over anger, bitterness, frustration, etc.?

CHAPTER 11

1. Death, grief, loss. How do you deal? How do you encourage others going through these times?

2. Our words seem trite, but God's Word brings comfort if given in right timing. I have already shared a favorite of mine Psalm 37. I also love Philippians 3:13–14. These verses were life verses for me when I was in college because they told me to forget what is in my past and encouraged me to push on. Sometimes we just need to get up in the morning and say things we are thankful for before we continue with our day. Do you have a routine that helps you move forward in a tough time? What helps you, and what advice could you give someone else going through trials?

3. It is encouraging to see changes within others we've prayed for, maybe even years later. Read Ezekiel 36:26.

CHAPTER 12

1. God rescues us. He chose to have His one and only Son die for us. God chose *me* to love. This took years to finally grasp. Write a list of praises to Him.

2. I love the Old Testament and God's promises. I think when I was young, I read more in the New Testament, but as I have gotten older, I can read the Old Testament over and over and can see that it is the basis for the New. Read Hosea 14, Deuteronomy 6, and Psalm 66.

3. Make a list of some people you can help in a tangible way this week. Maybe it is a widow or single mom that needs you to check on them. Or perhaps someone you could take a meal to or babysit for so they can have an evening out. We can be God's instrument to help change lives. Write your list. Pray about each person. *Go and do.*

CHAPTER 13

1. God has not left us or rejected us. I believe that is one reason He gave us His Word full of promises and hope. He has also shown us the stories of dozens of heroes of the faith that have held strong and stood their ground and those who fell into sin and did not trust, but He loved them anyway and gave them hope. Who is your favorite Bible hero and why?

2. Resolution. Somehow, we have to resolve to get past our pain or at least cope as we are going through it. Maybe you have not gone through a trial lately. But life happens, and I have learned that if we remain in the Word and fellowship with God and other believers, when something big hits, it is much easier to deal with the situation no matter how difficult. What are things that you do to strengthen your walk?

NICKI CORINNE WHITE
Put on a Heart of Compassion -- Colossians 3:12

CONTACT INFO

@NICKICORINNEWHITE

NICKICORINNEWHITE@GMAIL.COM

NICKICORINNE.COM

MYBLOG.NICKICORINNE.COM

ABOUT THE AUTHOR

Nicki Corinne White has a passion for studying and teaching God's Word. She has been leading Bible studies and discipling young women for many years. She is very involved in her local church with both children's ministry and women's ministry. She has a tender heart for those who are hurting and those who are new to church. Nicki hopes to be an encouragement to those around her by lending a listening ear, kind word, or a biblical reminder. She opens her home to share and serve others through hospitality on a regular basis and believes we are all called to do this. Nicki feels blessed to have been able to use her story and personal experience to encourage others, and she hopes to expand this ministry through her writing.

Nicki grew up in Snohomish, Washington, with her mom, dad, and sister Lisa. She was adopted at the age of one with her sister Lisa into the Maynard family. Nicki went to college at a small Christian liberal arts college in Southern California where she earned a bachelor's degree in Biblical Ministries. She met her husband, Craig, after graduating and was married two years later in 1984. After having their first three children, they moved to Boise, Idaho, where their fourth child was born. This is where they raised their children and made their home. Nicki has worked several jobs, including teaching, merchandizing, administrative work, and various artist projects. She enjoys spending time outdoors, painting, writing, and cheering on the Boise State Broncos and with her four children and five grandchildren.

NICKI CORINNE WHITE *ncw*

Put on a Heart of Compassion -- Colossians 3:12